Elizabeth Tudor

Portrait of Elizabeth I attributed to N. Hilliard, c. 1575.

Courtesy of the National Portrait Gallery, London.

Elizabeth Tudor

Portrait of a Queen

Lacey Baldwin Smith

THE LIBRARY OF WORLD BIOGRAPHY

J. H. PLUMB, GENERAL EDITOR

HUTCHINSON OF LONDON

IN ASSOCIATION WITH

JONATHAN CAPE

Hutchinson & Co (Publishers) Ltd
3 Fitzroy Square, London W1

London Melbourne Sydney Auckland
Wellington Johannesburg and agencies
throughout the world

First published in Great Britain 1976
© Lacey Baldwin Smith 1975

Printed in Great Britain by litho by The Anchor Press Ltd
and bound by Wm Brendon & Son Ltd
both of Tiptree, Essex

ISBN 0 09 126400 6

Contents

INTRODUCTION. The Queen of Addiction   3

ONE. The Favour of Heaven   11

TWO. Remember Old King Harry   17

THREE. What It Was to Be a Subject   33

FOUR. To Be a King and Wear a Crown   58

FIVE. Our Noble Phoenix   85

SIX. The Word of a Prince   118

SEVEN. Neither Hot nor Cold   150

EIGHT. Sometime So, Sometime No   169

NINE. Good Mistress — Dread Sovereign   193

Bibliographical Note   221

Index   225

Foreword

WHEN WE LOOK BACK at the past nothing, perhaps, fascinates us so much as the fate of individual men and women. The greatest of these seem to give a new direction to history, to mold the social forces of their time and create a new image, or open up vistas that humbler men and women never imagined. An investigation of the interplay of human temperament with social and cultural forces is one of the most complex yet beguiling studies a historian can make; men molded by time, and time molded by men. It would seem that to achieve greatness both the temperament and the moment must fit like a key into a complex lock. Or rather a master key, for the very greatest of men and women resonate in ages distant to their own. Later generations may make new images of them — one has only to think what succeeding generations of Frenchmen have made of Napoleon, or Americans of Benjamin Franklin — but this only happens because some men change the course of history and stain it with their own ambitions, desires, creations or hopes of a magnitude that embraces future generations like a miasma. This is particularly true of the great figures of religion, of politics, of war. The great creative spirits, however, are used by subsequent generations in a reverse manner — men and women go to them to seek hope or solace, or to confirm despair, reinterpreting the works of imagination or wisdom to ease them in their own desperate necessities, to beguile them with a sense of beauty or merely to draw from them strength and understanding. So this series of biographies tries in lucid, vivid, and dramatic narratives to explain the greatness of men and women, not only how they managed to secure their niche in the great pantheon of Time, but also why they have continued to fascinate subsequent generations. It may seem, therefore, that it is paradoxical for this series to contain living men and women, as well as the dead, but it is not so. We can recognize, in our own time, particularly in those whose careers are getting close to their final hours, men and women of indisputable greatness, whose position in history is secure, and about whom the legends and myths are beginning to sprout — for all great men and women become legends, all become in history larger than their own lives.

"I that was wont to behold her riding like Alexander, walking like Venus, the gentle wind blowing her fair hair about her pure cheeks like a nymph, sometimes sitting in the shade like a Goddess, sometimes playing like Orpheus — behold! the sorrow of this world once amiss hath bereaved me of all." So wrote Sir Walter Raleigh to a friend in a private letter after he was exiled from the Court by Elizabeth for secretly marrying. At the time Elizabeth I was old, wizened, bewigged, who could, on occasion, swear like a fishwife. Her teeth were gone and her breasts, bravely exposed, mere flaps. And yet there was nothing unusual in this ornate, extravagant, allegorical paean of praise to Elizabeth. It was the commonplace rhetoric of her courtiers and her poets. She was Diana, she was Cynthia, she was Astrea, the chaste moon goddess, the Virgin Queen second only to the Virgin Mother. In poems, in pageants, in elaborate chivalric jousts, Elizabeth I was constantly apostrophized in elaborate and esoteric allegory. Likewise in her portraits. The Privy Council, shortly after her accession, forebade unauthorized portraits of the Queen, and those which we now possess are as elaborate in their iconography as her poets' effusions are in allegory. The pearls in her hair, the rainbow in her hand, the ermine on her sleeve, speak in their private language of those enduring qualities with which her courtiers wished to endow her.

To those who could not read the complex language of emblems, the very extravagance of poetry or portrait projected a godlike image. And one that never aged. On her great progresses through London she was carried about like some strange barbaric goddess in her litter. The divinity that hedged a king was made visible to her subjects, but she symbolized more than mere chastity, virginity and regality. She also represented the purity of the Protestant religion, and the ever-growing self-confident nationalism of her subjects.

Behind the image, contrived, artificial, yet meaningful, was a strange, highly intelligent woman of complex temperament. Elizabeth I was strangely indecisive, yet she possessed a remarkable instinct for the dimension of time. Furthermore, the Queen was a very remarkable judge of the character of her statesmen servants — Burghley, Walsingham, the younger Cecil, who were trusted and maintained in power. Scold them she might, but she stayed loyal. Moved by male beauty, she never succumbed to it, and could bring herself to send her loved Essex to the block. Yet there was a very coarse streak in this accomplished woman. She could talk bawdy and romp indecorously with Robert Dudley. As a girl she had known nothing but treason, plot and civil war, and all the violence of religious strife. She herself had been near to death in the Tower. The fires of Smithfield had darkened the years of her young womanhood. She had been forced to prevaricate, to dissemble and, above all, to wait. Early experience strengthened the convolutions of her temperament. Indeed, she is far easier to grasp in her public image than in her private character.

Fortunately the public image was the one her subjects knew, and helped to bring a sense of unity and purpose to her nation. And she was singularly fortunate in her time. She was the last Tudor; until the execution of Mary, Queen of Scots, the one certain Protestant bulwark against the mounting tide of the Catholic Counter-Reformation. Patriotism and Protestantism, both deeply symbolized in her person and her office, were fused in her reign, and through the defeat of the Spanish Armada in 1588 bred an arrogant self-confidence in her nation. During her reign, too, the borderlands were secured and tied more tightly to the government in London. England, in spite of occasional rebellions and plots, experienced a security and peace which it had scarcely experienced for centuries. And so she was Gloriana as well as Astrea.

Fortunately for Elizabeth, too, the tide of the Renaissance swept through her court — music, poetry, the plays of Marlowe and Shakespeare, brought to English culture a brilliance that was entirely new. This flowering of culture was not distinct from Elizabeth, but an intimate part of her Court. Her learning, her appreciation of poetry and of music, of painting and of architecture, was as acute as any of her courtiers'. She was in every sense a princess of the Renaissance, a Minerva as well as Gloriana.

She became a legend in her own lifetime, adulated by her courtiers, venerated by her Parliaments, respected by her bitterest enemies. And for the sixteenth century that a mere woman should triumph so bordered on the miraculous. Hence the extravagant praise of Raleigh, and other court poets, becomes entirely comprehensible.

Yet because she was so iconlike a figure, so symbolic to her nation of English Protestantism and the successful fight against Spain, the woman was lost in the image of the Queen. Her reputation, enhanced by the follies and tragedies of the Stuarts, projected this image as an enduring part of English history. In consequence, to disentangle the reality from the legend is both complex and difficult. Even more difficult is to discern the true nature of this extraordinary woman, with her prevarications and evasions, who, at the same time, could rise to a superlative poetic rhetoric, and one that brought to her nation a sense of special destiny. So complex a character, so remarkable a triumph, requires a historian with deep psychological insight, as well as scholarship and analytical power — all qualities which Lacey Baldwin Smith displays in this remarkable biography.

— J. H. PLUMB

Elizabeth Tudor

INTRODUCTION

❧❧❧

The Queen of Addiction

Now death has extinguished envy and lighted up fame,
the felicity of her memory contends in a manner with
the felicity of her life.
— FRANCIS BACON, *On the Fortunate Memory of Elizabeth*

FAME, as Mark Twain said, is "a rough business. Shakespeare's dead, Dickens is dead, and I don't feel so good myself." Fame has been prodigal with Elizabeth I. Like Cleopatra she has become the "Queen of Addiction" who "makes hungry where most she satisfies." A quick glance at the British Museum's holdings gives a count — exclusive of lectures, special studies, characterizations, observations and polemics — of some sixty full-length biographies of the Virgin Queen in five different languages. Time has in no way dulled the appetite, and for the last fourteen years the average has been one new biography a year. The addict can read about Gloriana's health, girlhood, death, private life, love affairs and ghost; study her progresses, maids of honor, courtiers, parliaments, spies, rebellions, speeches and witticisms; sample her image in drama, poetry and French literature; and can even be told that she was the author of Shakespeare. The Queen has been called Bad Queen Bess, Good Queen Bess, The Protestant Queen, The Lonely Queen, The Maiden Queen, The Cankered Rose, A Tudor Wench and Elizabeth the Great, but most biographers have opted for just plain Elizabeth on the happy assumption that the world will always recognize Elizabeth Tudor by her first name.

No other woman, no other English sovereign, has been exposed to so much scrutiny. Over the centuries Gloriana's reputation has been extraordinarily durable and resilient, surviving not only Stuart antipathy, Catholic bias, eighteenth-century enlightenment, nineteenth-century liberalism and twentieth-century social-scientific research but also a growing mountain of historical documentation that has not substantially modified the nostalgic reconstructions which contemporaries wrote from personal memory.

Elizabeth left no cipher with which to unlock the secret of her personality, no diary, no memoirs, and almost no private letters. What has survived is an occasional intimate postscript to public letters generally drafted by the principal secretaries of state, a number of magnificent official speeches, a handful of poems of somewhat doubtful authenticity, an occasional prayer and an avalanche of sayings, witticisms and episodes, treasured (but often fabricated) by those who watched and recorded her every action. Where there is scanty evidence, there is endless debate. Elizabeth has been applauded or denounced on a host of improbable grounds. Oliver Cromwell, who stood for almost everything the Queen most abhorred, transformed her into a parliamentary heroine who had initiated the holy war with Spain which he and his Calvinist saints felt obliged to carry on — "Queen Elizabeth of famous memory: we need not be ashamed to call her so." In the eighteenth century David Hume, as might be predicted, was captivated "by the force of her mind." She was "endowed with a great command over her-self" and therefore "soon obtained an uncontrolled ascendant over her people." Elizabeth was the prince of reason, unfa-natical and rational, the proper precursor of the enlightened mind, but the romantics of the century, especially Doctor Johnson, could find no excuse for her "unrelenting cruelty" towards her cousin. "So unkind to my ancestress, the Queen of Scots" is the way Queen Victoria later put it.

The leading Whig historians of the nineteenth century had trouble making up their minds about Elizabeth: whether she was a great queen but a bad woman, or conversely an extraor-dinary female but a bad sovereign. Thomas Macaulay could not forgive her the "haughty and imperious" way she handled Parliament, her disdain for free speech and her failure to an-ticipate the nineteenth century's more tolerant stand on reli-gion, but for all her deficiencies he accepted her as "a great woman." John Lingard reversed the argument. As the most temperate and scholarly of the Catholic historians of his day, he magnanimously acknowledged Bess as a brilliant monarch — "among the greatest and most fortunate of princes" — but he branded her a hopelessly flawed female: vain, parsimonious and of doubtful sexual morals. Morals were forever getting in the way of the Victorian view of Gloriana. Bishop Mandell Creighton actually dismissed the Tudors as so "awful" that he did not "think that anyone ought to read the history of the sixteenth century," but fortunately this did not prevent him from writing one of the best short biographies of the Queen. Despite the fact that there were "many things in Elizabeth which we could have wished otherwise," Creighton proudly claimed that "she saw what England might become, and nursed it into the knowledge of its power." Viewed from the pinnacle of Victorian Britain, the Queen was irresistible. She was a crucial part of that manifest destiny which had brought the island to its happy state of constitutional, social, economic and imperial perfection, and not even J. A. Froude, with all his suspicions of Gloriana both as a monarch and a woman, was willing to disown her; so much that was great had happened under her administration. "Princes," he confessed, "who are credited on the wrong side with the evils which happen in their reigns have a right in equity to the honour of the good."

As the importance of organized religion and strict morality have receded, the twentieth century's taste for Elizabeth has changed but not diminished. With few exceptions she has been treated more sympathetically because less has been expected of her. Power politics, the awareness of the juxtaposition between men and events, knowledge of the environmental factors which condition both mind and body, and a greater willingness to accept inconsistencies and contradictions have produced a richer, more complex and more humane portrait of the Queen. "Great but difficult to live with" sums up the current vogue.

So why yet another biography? In part the answer is self-evident, Elizabeth is indeed an addiction. In part, it involves two other fascinations: the impact of personality on politics and the nature of success. In the midst of change, crisis and conflict, the twentieth century is obsessed with the quality of leadership, even to the point of endowing university chairs to study how our leaders stumble into decisions of no one's making. Elizabeth constitutes one of the most unique and baffling examples of what might be called the metaphysics of political success, for the quality and measure of her achievement were purchased at the price of endless failure — failure on the part of men and women who would not or could not respond to her particular style of political control, and failure on her own part to resolve most of the major problems of her reign.

The astute reader will quickly detect the extent to which

this brief biographical excursion is dependent upon the host of authors who have gone before, in particular upon Sir John Neale, the dean of modern Elizabethan studies. At the same time credit belongs to a far more distant past: to the writers of Elizabeth's own day — Sir John Harington, Sir Robert Naunton, Sir Francis Bacon, William Camden and John Clapham — and above all to the Queen herself, whose final words to Parliament contain the riddle which this essay seeks to resolve: "by looking into the course which I have ever holden . . . in governing . . . you may more easily discern in what kind of sympathy my care to benefit hath corresponded with your inclination to obey, and my caution with your merit."

The Tudors: 1485–1603

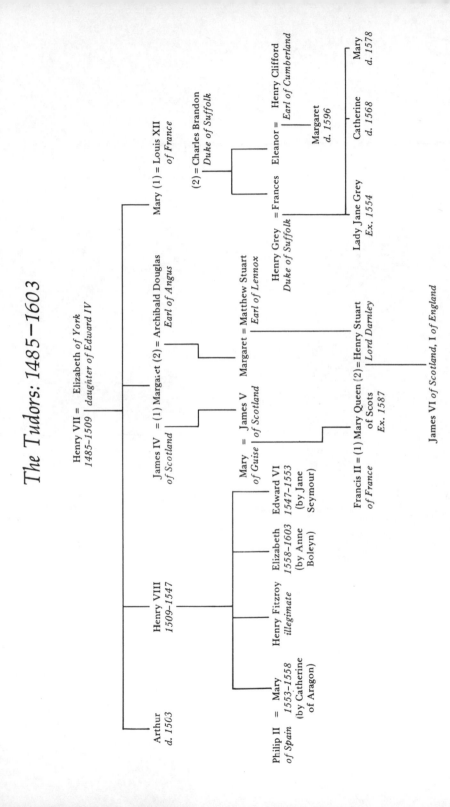

ONE

The Favour of Heaven

God preserve her Majesty long to reign over us by some
unlooked-for miracle, for I cannot see by natural reason
that her Highness goeth about to provide for it.
— FRANCIS WALSINGHAM *to* THOMAS SMITH, 1572

"INIMICAL FORTUNE, envious of all good and ever revolving
human affairs"; these are the first recorded words that Elizabeth Tudor wrote. At eleven Elizabeth misinterpreted her
stars, but the child's conviction that all mankind is chained to
fortune's wheel raises the essential mystery of the Queen's
career: why did destiny smile upon a lady who defied all the
canons of good government, equivocated, delayed, drifted and
habitually changed her mind, yet somehow transformed every
defect into a magic that has survived four hundred years? She
stands as an exception to every rule of political success, a
thorn in the side of time and an infuriating puzzle to all who
sought to serve her.

Gloriana did very little that can be recorded in parchment
and stone. She was a bespangled female of uncertain temper
possessed of immense personal magnetism and an unerring

sense of style, who played chess with men's emotions, pursued policies which seemed dangerously anachronistic and egocentric to the overwhelming body of her advisers, and who unmercifully traded upon the perishable goods of life: her sex and her stamina. Yet she became a legend in her own day, a talisman for her kingdom against the hordes of hell, and a disturbing witness to later generations that indecision, half-measures and outmoded concepts of state, when placed upon the wheel of "ever revolving human affairs" and judged by historic hindsight, can engender political success just as readily as the most immaculate and updated scheme of idealist, social planner and statesman.

Hindsight is of course the rub, and success itself a paradox. Life as it is actually lived is more often than not dull, despairing and deceptive; only in the recording does it take on the color of pageantry and is proclaimed a success or failure. What kind of success would the most devoted lieutenant today project for his leader if he had to write, as did Sir Thomas Smith, that "this irresolution doth weary and kill her ministers, destroy her actions and overcome all good designs and counsels"? Over and over the same refrain can be heard from the Queen's advisers and servants who could foresee nothing but disaster because their mistress could not make up her mind. "For the love of God, Madam," exploded Sir Francis Walsingham, "let not the cure of your diseased estate hang any longer in deliberation." In more perplexed tones, the Queen's Principal Secretary Sir William Cecil wrote, "what her Majesty will determine to do only God I think knoweth." As for the young Earl of Essex, the Bess of his generation had grown "no less crooked in mind than in body" and "wrangles with our action for no cause but because it is in hand." The picture of Elizabeth is not pretty and substantiates the worst male chauvinist fears of "wavering women's wit." Indeed, it was a source of considerable comfort to the sovereigns of Europe to know that not much could be "expected from a country governed by a Queen," and even loyal William Cecil could find little to dispel his innate pessimism that "the end will be monstrous." Yet all the doleful prophecies, bitter criticisms and tears shed for chances lost went for naught. Gloriana's diseased estate did not languish and die. Instead, a miracle took place: Elizabeth lived, the assassin's blade was blunted, the Queen's enemies were confounded, and her crablike diplomacy proved sufficient to keep her kingdom secure and prosperous. In joyous if exaggerated words Speaker Christopher Yelverton looked back over almost forty years of brilliant achievement and sang Eliza's praises: "You behold other kingdoms distracted into factions, distressed with wars, swarming with rebellions, and imbrued with blood. Yours — almost only yours — remaineth calm without tempest and quiet without dissension, notwithstanding all the desperate and devilish devices of the Romish crew. . . ."

Yelverton's language in 1597 was thought somewhat "too full of flattery, too curious and tedious," and displayed that peculiarly English penchant for ignoring civil war in Ireland. Nevertheless the Speaker stated an important truth. Elizabeth succeeded in living through four decades of rather shoddy history without forfeiting her glamour, and the best minds of her century were proved wrong. It was an indisputable political feat to become a living myth. Most heroes of state are safely placed in their tombs before they acquire the odor of political sanctity, their canonization the product of nostalgia for a dead past and the need to delude the mind with what-might-have-been. There is nothing more fatal to reputation than survival, yet somehow Elizabeth managed it. For most men there seemed to be only one possible solution: fortune far from being inimical had avowed herself to be English. Almost without dissent contemporaries spoke of that felicitous destiny which "was so constant and flourishing," of "good fortune, never wavering, which accompanied her clear up to her death," and of "the favour of heaven as constant as [it was] impenetrable." Even Elizabeth felt that modesty obliged her to admit that she could not "attribute those haps and good success to my device without detracting much from the divine providence; nor challenge to my private commendation what is only due to God's eternal glory." After all, she was only a woman, and it was not seemly to claim too much credit for such a successful dominion over men.

The gods move in mysterious ways, and for an age deeply aware of the doubtfulness of fortune and the caprice of heaven, it was sufficient to accept God's bounty and leave the explanation in divine hands. But even in the sixteenth century some men felt that there was far too much good luck to ascribe it all to providence. As Francis Bacon observed, it was difficult to believe that "so happy a fortune [could] . . . fall to the lot of any but such as besides being singularly sustained and nourished by the divine favour are also in some measure by their own virtue the makers of such fortune for themselves."

Someone had to be responsible, and over the course of years two choices have emerged — Elizabeth or her ministers. In her own day it was only politic to give the Queen the benefit of the doubt, and publicly at least most men would have agreed with the panegyric of the Venetian Ambassador, who pronounced that of all the princes in the world "she was the most prudent in governing, the most active in all business, the most clear-sighted in seeing events, and the most resolute in seeing her resolutions carried into effect . . . in a word, [she] possessed, in the highest degree, all the qualities which are required in a great prince." Later historians have echoed and reechoed those sentiments, and in their hands Elizabeth has become a cool, calculating votaress who "in maiden meditation, fancy free," refused to be stampeded into unwise actions. Prevarication, procrastination and postponement became the artful instruments of the perfect Renaissance prince who alone knew that time was on her side. At the other end of the spectrum are those who note Sir William Cecil's laconic comment that "with some long laborious persuasion her Majesty was induced to agree. . . ." Presumably initiative and concept rested with the Queen's Principal Secretary, and if fortune smiled upon the kingdom it was not because of Elizabeth's "great judgment" but because Walsingham and Cecil, Howard and Drake, Leicester and Knollys were present to guide their sovereign's fumbling hand and circumvent her anachronistic ways.

The debate is, of course, a specious one. We are not confronted with the lady or the tiger: on one side a wise, enigmatic inactivity based on careful thought, and on the other a royal indecision deftly converted into continuous and sensible policy by far-seeing ministers. In a working monarchy where the prince possesses total liberty to select both men and policies ultimate responsibility must reside with royalty, but such a paradigm presumes a freedom of choice and a selection of options which Elizabeth, both as a woman and as a sovereign, neither expected nor desired. She was a slave to events and to those she appointed to serve her. The final outcome of policy was always as much the result of decisions made in haste, ignorance or exhaustion as it was the product of rational planning on the part of Queen or councillor.

With Elizabeth one is reduced to speaking in terms of paradoxes, of a paragon of procrastination, a mirror of hesitation and a master of indecision, for the excellent reason that whatever it was she did or did not do seems to have worked, to have been in the eyes of history blessed with success. So still the query stands — what made Gloriana successful? Providence or her own prudence? Success may be an illusion — a trick of historical lighting — and one may run the risk of destroying it by too close scrutiny; like royalty it cannot stand the daylight lest the magic vanish. But that rare felicity with which the Queen ruled for nearly forty-five years involves more than historical fantasy. Fortune, chance, providence and the sheer perversity of events played their part; so also did personality. It has been said that men shape their own destinies but never exactly as they choose. Elizabeth put it more effectively. As her long life was drawing to a close, she said to Lord Charles Howard: "My lord, I am tied with a chain of iron about my neck." The first and strongest link of that chain was forged when on a Sunday afternoon between three and four o'clock, the seventh of September, 1533, she was born Elizabeth Tudor.

TWO

Remember Old King Harry

And what is Time but shadows that were cast
By these storm-sculptured stones while centuries fled?
— SIEGFRIED SASSOON, "What Is Stonehenge?"

"IN HUMAN BEINGS as in horses, there is something to be said for the hereditary principle." Genetically the rule may hold good for horses but it breaks down with humans — the species is too promiscuous in its sexual habits and too liable to wishful thinking in the recording of its pedigrees — but Elizabeth believed implicitly in the principle, and historically speaking the single most important circumstance of her life was the fact that she was Henry Tudor's daughter. Neither the taint of bastardy nor the frailty of her sex could diminish the claims of royal blood. Throughout her life this fact was never forgotten, and the Earl of Sussex, even as he conducted the Princess to her prison cell in the Tower, was at pains to caution his colleagues: "Let us take heed, my Lords, that we do not go beyond our commission, for she was our King's daughter."

The Earl's warning, spoken seven years after Henry had

gone to his tomb, was not only politic recognition that Elizabeth in 1554 was heir presumptive to the throne, but it was also witness to the potency of the old King's memory. Spiritually as well as biologically Henry VIII was parent to the daughter, and it was no accident that subjects who watched as the young Queen rode to her coronation in January of 1559 should have shouted "Remember old King Harry the Eighth." Nobody, especially Elizabeth, could forget that "serene and invincible prince" whose dalliance had planted and whose conscience had nourished the seeds of the English Reformation.

It is difficult to do justice to a sovereign whom some wished in hell while others regarded as "the rarest man who lived in his time," to a father of whom it could be said in one breath that he was "a most gentle gentleman" and in the next "the most dangerous and cruel man in the world," and to a husband whose second wife, minutes before she died by the executioner's sword, could "pray for the life of the King, my sovereign lord and yours, who is one of the best princes on the face of the earth and who has always treated me so well that better could not be." In the year of Elizabeth's birth Henry was forty-two, still fair of face, graceful of step and hard of frame, a magnificent specimen of a man and a mighty monarch who had risked his soul and staked his kingdom to marry Anne Boleyn. Though there is some uncertainty as to the exact date on which Anne promised to be "bonair and buxsom at bed and at board," few people then or now believed Elizabeth's assertion that "her mother would not cohabit with the King save as his wife." The chronicler Ralph Holinshed assigns the marriage to 14 November, 1532, but the more popular date is January 25, 1533, months after Mistress Anne had given herself up "body and heart" to her "loyal servitor" and probably timed to the biological evidence of her matrimonial worth.

The story of that romance and the papal dragon that Henry

slew for the sake of his true love is an oft-told tale in which grave matters of state and what Harry himself called "the bowels of his conscience and heart" intermingled in proportions which are still hotly debated. The "dart of love" that pierced so deeply the King's heart is evident enough. Sometime during 1526 Henry fell in love with a dark-eyed, black-haired wench whose wit, vivacity and animal attraction for her royal admirer more than compensated for her merchant blood and unexpected refusal to oblige her prince until he had presented her with a crown. After six interminable years of fruitless diplomacy with Rome and the danger that her unsatisfied lover might look elsewhere for favors more easily purchased, Anne decided to compromise. In September of 1532 she accepted the title of Marquis of Pembroke and a yearly income of £1,000 and climbed into the King's bed. Six years of unrequited love is a long time by any standards, and it is doubtful whether Henry would have been able to marshal the necessary patience or self-restraint had it not been for two other factors — the acute dynastic difficulties of his house and the prick of a particularly susceptible conscience.

The need for a legitimate male heir to secure the succession and to assure Henry a place in the memory of the world to his "perpetual reknown and fame and to the glory of Almighty God" was inherent in the nature of sixteenth-century monarchy. Nothing was more dangerous to the safety of the realm than too few heirs or too many royal bratlings; either case was an invitation to civil war in a kingdom in which political loyalties were still perilously parochial and personal. In 1526 the future looked ominous. The King's Spanish wife, Catherine of Aragon, was fat, sterile and forty-two, and the unsatisfactory choice for the succession lay between Mary Tudor, female but legitimate, and Henry Fitzroy, male but illegitimate. Sexually and politically the situation was not without solution. Catherine's daughter, the Princess Mary, could have been married to her first cousin, James V of Scotland, and their offspring named heir to the English throne; or Henry could have opted for any one of a number of ingenious proposals suggested by a pontiff desperate to oblige his dutiful English son and Defender of the Faith. The simplest solution would have been for Catherine to have retired voluntarily to a nunnery, but barring this happy event, His Holiness was willing to bless adultery by legitimizing the offspring of Anne and Henry, to sanction the marriage of Mary to her illegitimate half-brother, or even to permit bigamy. In short, from the perspective of Rome almost anything was preferable to an enforced annulment of the King's marriage to the Queen.

Some form of amicable arrangement might have been devised except for the King's conscience. In part the issue was a matter of strict legality about which the King was always a stickler. Henry was an expert on God's law as it had been revealed in Scripture and interpreted by the church fathers, and he was not willing to accept two wives at a time even with papal approval. It would not have satisfied his conscience. Moreover, he was determined that any future offspring he sired should be unimpeachably legitimate, and this necessitated a legal annulment. More important was the King's conviction that the solution to his dynastic difficulties lay not in Rome but in his soul. Like most of his subjects he believed that every good and every evil came from God in proportions commensurate with man's actions on earth. "I am the Lord Your God" and "if ye walk contrary unto me, and will not hearken unto me" then will I "break the pride of your power" and "make your heaven as iron, and your earth as brass" (Lev. 26:14–21). Henry put it more egotistically if more prosaically: he could not "see that there is any faith in the whole world, save in me, and therefore God Almighty, who knows this, prospers my affairs." If he conformed to the prescribed ritual, followed the exact formula, and testified "his zeal for the faith" with all the "resources of his mind and body," God would reward him with fame in this life and salvation in the next. Should the deity withhold his blessings, then it was time to look for the cause of divine wrath.

When Catherine of Aragon disappointed her royal husband by failing to secure the succession in the male line, there could be only one explanation — "All such males as I have received of the Queen died immediately after they were born; so that I fear the punishment of God in that behalf." The source of the Lord's anger lay in Leviticus 20:21 — "If a man shall take his brother's wife, it is an unclean thing . . . they shall be childless." In marrying Catherine, Henry had done exactly what God's law forbade, for his Queen had been for five months the wife of his brother Arthur. It was all ancient history and in 1509 a papal dispensation had nullified any biblical prohibition when Henry had married his sister-in-law, but now eighteen years later the King perceived God's hand in the death of all but one girl child of that union. Neither a papal dispensation nor his wife's oath that she had come to his bed "a true maid without touch of man" could hide the evidence of sin. It was no longer simply a question of a male heir; if Henry's place in paradise was to be reserved for him and his kingdom guarded against the vengeance of heaven, his marriage had to be annulled. As Henry said, the truth was so manifest that it "ought to be allowed and received not as a matter doubtful . . . but as a plain, determined and discussed verity of the true understanding of God's word and law which all Christians must follow and obey." Ultimately it was conscience, not politics or sex, that made Henry so certain of the justice of his cause that even an angel descending from heaven would not have been "able to persuade him to the contrary."

At first no one seriously considered the possibility that a divorce could not be engineered. Customarily popes were understanding about the dynastic needs of kings, but in 1527 Henry and his conscience suddenly found themselves caught in a three-way vise; Catherine would not resign her marital rights to a commoner or forfeit the claims of her daughter as heir to the throne, Anne would not gratify her lover unless he presented her with a marriage certificate, and the pontiff could not give him a legal separation. Clement VII was in an impossible situation, for the delicate balance of power between Valois France and the Hapsburg empire on which his political independence rested had been hopelessly upset in 1525 by the Emperor Charles's crushing victory over Francis I at the Battle of Pavia. By 1527 France had been thrown out of Italy and his Holiness had become a Hapsburg chaplain determined "to live and die an Imperialist," a decision of no great import to Henry except for the embarrassing fact that his wife was Charles's great-aunt, and the Emperor believed strongly in family solidarity.

For three years Henry alternately threatened, cajoled and negotiated, only to be made ridiculous when in the summer of 1529 Cardinal Campeggio, who had been commissioned by the Pope to try the divorce in London, received secret instructions to "decide nothing, for the Emperor is victorious and we cannot afford to provoke him," and to adjourn the case to Rome. If Henry was ever to rid himself of his wife he had to stop Catherine from appealing her case to the Vatican, the highest spiritual authority in Christendom. And so it was that the King's "Great Matter" contained within it the seeds of a religious revolution, for only by the denial of papal authority and the transformation of an English king into a pope in England could Henry's divorce be legalized, his offspring made legitimate and his vexed conscience eased.

Henry was "far from reckless." Like his daughter Elizabeth, he disliked making up his mind or being catapulted into irrevocable decisions, but by January of 1553 time was running out. He had married Anne and she was now two months pregnant. If he was going to save himself from bigamy and his love-child from bastardy, he had seven months in which to be done with Catherine. Once the decision had been forced upon him, events moved rapidly. In April by a stroke of the parliamentary pen it was decreed that all spiritual cases "shall be from henceforth . . . definitely adjudged and determined within the King's jurisdiction and authority" and "not elsewhere." A month later the sovereign appeared before the archdiocesan court of Canterbury to receive final judgment from a prelate who had been carefully picked for his loyalty to the King's cause. It came as no surprise to hear that Henry's marriage had been for twenty-four years invalid and that he was free to marry whomever he chose. On June 1, six years of patience triumphed. Against every prognostication, against the wishes of certainly more than half the population and in defiance of the collective conscience of Christendom, Anne Boleyn was presented with her crown. Nothing more could now be done except to await the fruits of the King's labors and the blessings of heaven.

Possibly no child was ever a greater disappointment to her parents than was Elizabeth, but for the time being Henry brazened it out. As the Spanish Ambassador said, when this King "decides for an undertaking he goes the whole length." His Queen was healthy, she had proved her fertility, and if God saw fit a robust boy would follow. Henry did not comment on what would happen if God should once again break the pride of his power. Instead, he announced the arrival of that "high and mighty Princess of England, Elizabeth," and paid for a proper christening for a royal daughter. It was significant, however, that he did not bother to attend the ceremony.

Even now, almost four hundred and fifty years after the event, it is tempting to say that Henry did it all himself: "Surrounded by faint hearts and fearful minds he neither faltered nor failed" in his purpose of transforming his kingdom into "an empire . . . governed by one supreme head and king" who was imbued by God with "plenary, whole and entire power." The principle of the nation-state above which stands no higher authority was implicit in the legislation denying Catherine and all other subjects the right of appeal to Rome. Once voiced it was only a matter of time until Parliament fulfilled the internal logic of the King's policy and smashed the essential spiritual and temporal duality of medieval Christendom by joining God and Caesar into a single omnipotent figure — "king, emperor and pope in his dominion." In November of 1534, fourteen months after Elizabeth's birth, Parliament gave formal recognition to a new-found political and theological truth: by the Act of Supremacy the King was to be accepted as "Supreme Head of the Church of England." The sixteenth century was content to give Henry full credit for the achievement, "yielding him thanks even in his sepulchre," and Elizabeth Tudor agreed entirely: her father was the one sovereign to whom she was willing to take second place. Years after the old King's death, when she herself had grown wise in the ways of monarchy, the Queen informed her Commons that of all the princes who had cared for them and loved them only her father "whom in the duty of a child I must regard, and to whom I must acknowledge myself far shallow" had worked harder than she had in safeguarding the kingdom and preventing "danger to come."

The fiction always remained that in the second Tudor there was "not only a king to be obeyed but an idol to be worshipped," but Henry himself did relatively little to achieve his ends. The parliamentary architect of the break with Rome was Thomas Cromwell, not the King. More important, it is doubtful whether Henry, an exceedingly conventional gentleman, would ever have risked his soul in defiance of Rome had not the ancient church already been seriously compromised with the current of educated opinion running heavily against it. The old ecclesia with its elegant gilded head in Rome, its tangled vested interests and worldly cynicism, its lawyers and tax collectors, its fat abbots and ignorant priests, its rich pluralists and greedy pardoners was the subject of ridicule and criticism.

Anti-clericalism, especially anti-papalism, was nothing new, and the old church might have continued successfully to ignore Erasmian laughter, scholarly scorn and secular ribaldry had it not been for that extraordinarily vital and explosive spiritual response to the guilt and degradation of the whole world known as the Reformation. The inner dynamism that induced monks to hurl their inkpots at the devil, soldiers to commit unspeakable atrocities in the name of God's Truth, and visionaries to reform church and state in the image of Christ's sacrifice was scarcely a decade old when Henry determined upon his divorce. Small in number but fervent in their commitment to God's word, those fortunate few who found "marvelous comfort and quiet" in Scripture supplied the militancy and idealism necessary to the King's purpose. They applauded the break with Rome as the constitutional prelude to a sweeping religious revival which would purge the new ecclesia not only of popery but also of spiritual apathy and perversion. Henry had little respect for these zealous reformers. He was suspicious of their inordinate faith in God's mercy which led them to do what was right simply because they believed themselves to be filled with divine grace, and he was only too aware that Protestantism could rob "princes and prelates of all power and authority." But much as the new Supreme Head disliked the religious radicals, he was dependent upon them. If the King's supremacy were not to "lie post alone, hidden in the acts of parliament," he required propagandists and preachers who really did believe that the Bishop of Rome was the whore of Babylon. Above all else he needed men who would spread the gospel that "the word of God is to obey the King and not the bishop of Rome." Unless the dictum was planted deeply in every subject's heart, Henry's crown would never again sit securely upon his head.

The Reformation intensified but it did not cause the doctrine of royal omnipotence or the divinity of kings. For years the crown had been intent upon destroying rival political loyalties and forging a single mystical unit composed of the prince and his right-thinking subjects. The English Reformation was simply the culmination of the creed: one king, one law, one faith. If Henry's realm was really an empire then the independence of the old church along with feudal privilege and private law had to give way to royal authority. Medieval monarchs had always been divine but that divinity had been shared with the church and the baronage. By Henry's reign, however, a qualitative as well as a quantitative distinction was emerging: The divinity of kings outshone all other kinds of sanctity, for the prince alone spoke for the deity. He was a "king among the stars," a "lion among beasts," and a "God on earth." Every subject, great or small, was expected "to forsake father, mother, kindred, wife and child, in respect of preserving the prince." Elizabeth was too young during her father's lifetime to know exactly what that doctrine meant in terms of personal sacrifice and tragedy, but her sister Mary did. The Princess's mother had been discarded, her own birthright denied, and the faith into which she had been born outlawed by the will of a sovereign father who was also her absolute lord and master. Mary's final humiliation came in 1536 when she was forced to acknowledge publicly her mother's marriage to be incestuous and her father to be Supreme Head of the Church. "For mine own opinion," she meekly wrote the King's Vicar General in Matters Spiritual, "I assure you I have none at all but such as I shall receive from him who hath my whole heart in his keeping, that is, the King's most gracious highness, my most benign father, who shall imprint in the same, touching these matters and all other what his inestimable virtue, high wisdom and excellent learning shall think convenient. . . ."

Henry spoke for God, and simple logic demanded that royal wisdom take precedent over the fond fancies of mere subjects. Elizabeth was forever fettered to the righteousness of her father's will and the special prudence of his wisdom, for she was the product of that conscience which accorded so well with God's design. To have rejected the justice of his actions or the divinity of his person would have been to deny herself and her own special relationship to God and history. Ultimately it was Henry's will, if not his intellect, that brought about the divorce and the break with Rome. In the eyes of Christendom he alone was responsible, and if he were proved wrong, of all the souls involved in schism his would burn most fiercely in hell. With that knowledge Elizabeth was born, raised and died.

"The court, like heaven, examines not the anger of princes" but "shines upon them on whom the king dost shine, smiles if he smiles, declines if he declines." For two years and five months Anne and her baby continued to bask in the royal sunlight, and the full meaning of the break with Rome was spitefully dramatized when that "cursed bastard," the Lady Mary, stripped of her title of Princess of Wales, was appointed maid of honor to Anne Boleyn's daughter and ordered to address her half-sister as the Princess Elizabeth. Then abruptly "inimical fortune" destroyed the Queen even more swiftly than it had elevated her. On 29 January, 1536, she was prematurely delivered of a stillborn male child. It was her second miscarriage in two years and ominous proof that God had once again withdrawn his favor from his anointed lieutenant on earth.

Behind the facade of divine omnipotence resided a rather timid and emotional man whose powers of self-deception kept abreast of the demands of his royal office. After a lifetime of cloaking every action with ceremonial make-believe and elevating even his most intimate and biological urges into a mystique of idol worship, it is not surprising if "Harry with the crown" lost his ability to distinguish between what was real and what was fake, or that his conscience fell victim to the self-deception that surrounded royalty and guarded him from the hell of doubting his own good intentions. It was not difficult for the King to believe the monstrous charges of mass adultery and incest leveled at his Queen, and he thanked his God for having rescued him from the "accursed whore." That Catherine of Aragon had conveniently died the previous December and that there was another lady waiting in the wings ready to test her fecundity only helped to make the King's sense of self-righteousness the more potent and urgent. If Henry could sire a male heir by Jane Seymour, no one, not even the Emperor Charles, could call that child illegitimate. Therefore Anne had to go. She was attainted for high treason and executed along with her brother George on May 19, 1536, and next day Henry took to himself a new wife, who alone of all his spouses dutifully bore him a son. Though she died of it, in October of 1537 she presented her delighted husband with that godly imp, Prince Edward. The effect on Anne Boleyn's daughter was instantaneous. The Catholic world had always referred to Elizabeth as "the concubine's little bastard"; now by Act of

Parliament her illegitimacy was made a statutory as well as a theological fact; like her sister, she was simply the Lady Elizabeth.

Before he was finished Henry went through three more wives, but the vicissitudes of the King's matrimonial escapades and the tumultuous doings at his court had little effect on a child who rarely went to London or saw her father. Since no one expected Elizabeth to become queen, it is not surprising that we know almost nothing about her during the remaining years of the old King's life. She was short of clothing, had trouble with her baby teeth, sent New Year's gifts to her brother Edward, grew fond of her sister Mary, and proved to be a matrimonial dud because, as Henry was informed, she lacked the necessary dynastic quality to be married to a real prince. The last of her father's queens, Catherine Parr, brought a certain degree of domestic bliss to court. She reconciled her husband to his daughters and befriended his children, mothering the little Prince, interesting Mary in Erasmus's *Paraphrases* and exposing Elizabeth to the tenets of humanistic piety.

The first thirteen years of Elizabeth's life were spent on the sidelines of politics, watching the human tragedies of those years unfold, and learning that Henry's wrath was death. Her mother, her uncle, her stepmother Catherine Howard and her poet cousin the Earl of Surrey, all died on the block because they had wronged the King her father. During those years, as she herself said, she did not spend her "time altogether idly," but underwent a rigorous intellectual training that served her well for the rest of her life. Her religious education was free from medieval scholastic pedantry, tempered on one side by her stepmother's Christian devotionalism and hardened on the other by the stern morality of the Book of Proverbs with its injunction to fear God and keep His commandments. First William Grindal, then Roger Ascham and John Cheke drilled her in classical languages, history, and "moral learning collected out of such authors as did best conduce to the institution of Princes." She learned to notice "any obscure or wrong word" and developed a lasting admiration for the metaphor as a literary and oratorical device. The training was exacting and intensive, and until the end of her days Elizabeth belabored her ministers with the same high stylistic standards, tightening their syntax, changing their phraseology, insisting on precise definitions and goading the overworked Sir Francis Walsingham into the exasperated explosion that he wished to God "her Majesty could be content to refer these things to them that can best judge of them as other princes do." There was no doubt that the pupil was sharp. She mastered Greek, could extemporize in Latin, spoke French and Italian fluently, and most important of all, was taught or inherited a flair for words which as Queen she used to obscure her true meaning in honeyed phrases and wrap her thoughts in verbal brilliance. As Roger Ascham said, she was his "brightest star." There was no false modesty about the attainment, and she frankly wrote her brother Edward that "for her face, I grant, I might well blush" but "the mind I shall never be ashamed to present." Forty years later she was still proud of her intellectual achievement and complacently announced that "few that be no professors have read more."

 Despite her bastardy, Elizabeth was a royal lady. The purpose of her education was not merely to enrich the spirit and quicken the intellect but also to steep the soul in duty and drill the mind in the deportment becoming a virgin and a princess. Young ladies were expected "to be wary in their words, and weighty in their writings," as well as courteous in their carriage and gracious in their gestures, but such womanly reserve had also to be leavened with the confidence and authority that goes with rank. Edward noted no more than the obvious when he wrote his sister, after their father's death, that she did not need his consolation "because from your learning you know what you ought to do. . . ." If as a child and a subject Elizabeth was expected to order herself "lowly and reverently" to all her betters, as a king's daughter she had every right to be "proud and disdainful." There was no more need for false humility about her royal station than about her intelligence. She was inordinately proud of both, and when she had learned to display the one and discipline the other, "then shall be séen her father's daughter."

Henry died on January 28, 1547. He had lived and now he sought to die by the creed that "all order standeth in ruling and obeying." To the end the men around him continued to obey, partly from habit and mental conditioning, partly from fear of being read out of the King's testament which established the blueprint of the future. By that document Henry willed his throne as if no hint of illegitimacy had ever touched his dynasty: to Edward, Mary and Elizabeth in that order. Then he did something which was to cause endless debate in later decades. Faced with the unlikely possibility that all his children might die childless, he settled the succession on the heirs of his younger sister, Mary Duchess of Suffolk, and ignored the Stuart and Douglas descendants of his elder sister, Margaret Queen of Scotland. Henry's will was more than a title of inheritance or a declaration that he intended to die in the ancient faith, secure in the blessings of the Virgin Mary and "the holy company of heaven." It was an instrument of government which established a council of regency, composed of eighteen "entirely beloved councillors" empowered to rule in the name of his young son. Edward was enjoined never "to change, molest, trouble nor disquiet" his advisers, and Elizabeth and Mary were informed that should they marry without the consent of the council, they would be barred from the succession.

Though his body was in the tomb, Henry, it seemed, was determined that his soul should go marching on. His awe-inspiring image had been preserved by Holbein on the wall of the Privy Chamber for all to see and worship, and there a frail, worried little boy of nine contemplated that icon of majesty and reminded himself of the words stenciled across his own portrait: "Imitate your father, the greatest man in the world. Surpass him, and none will surpass you!" It was a frightful responsibility.

THREE

What It Was to Be a Subject

How chary ought all Virgins to be? how carefull
and cautious in all their deportments?
— THOMAS HEYWOOD, *A Curtaine Lecture, 1638*

EVEN ONE SET of in-laws poses difficulties; Henry, extravagant
man, endured six, of which the Hapsburgs and the Howards
had proved the most troublesome. Now, even as he lay dying,
his brother-in-law Edward Seymour, Earl of Hertford, con-
spired to overthrow his testament because it vested power in
a council of regency in which the Earl was merely one among
eighteen equals. The century was far too authoritarian in its
instincts and the issues facing the new reign far too weighty to
permit cumbersome majority rule by a headless council. It was
essential that a single voice speak as nurse and guardian for a
kingdom where the Prince was a child. Within four days of
Henry's death Hertford, as senior uncle to the King, was elevated by the "unanimous" vote of his colleagues to the office of
Lord Protector and Governor of the King's Body. Edward Seymour's vanity, nourished by his sharp-tongued and ambitious
wife, was immensely flattered by the wealth and titles thrust

upon him — especially the dukedom of Somerset which brought his private income to £7,400 a year — but the new Duke might not have been so anxious to set aside the insulting terms of his brother-in-law's will had he appreciated the full magnitude of Henry's legacy.

The Church of England, that popeless anomaly on which the royal supremacy had been grafted, was a religious deformity intravenously kept alive by the dogma that Henry Tudor spoke for God. Personal loyalty to the Prince, fortified by fear of statutes written in blood and grounded upon an atavistic dread that God's lieutenant on earth could miraculously detect the malice hidden in disloyal hearts, was the keystone of the Tudor monarchy. The Duke in contrast was simply the King's maternal uncle, no more than a man of "fit age" who stood *in loco parentis* to royalty. No divinity graced his office, no Tudor blood filled his veins and no charisma won him the hearts of Englishmen. Once the magnetism and authority of the old King was gone, Henry's loving and obedient subjects forsook their commendable sobriety and charity for a host of licentious religious notions and dangerous social doctrines. The crucial question after 1547 was whether anyone could fill the void, whether anyone could persuade Englishmen to forgo immediate religious and political profit for ultimate social gain and infuse the body politic with a new sense of unity and purpose. Four times the effort would be made — first under the Lord Protector, then in 1550 when Northumberland seized power, again in 1553 on the succession of Mary, and finally by Elizabeth. Only with the last attempt were the human, ideological and social elements sufficiently fusible to produce the formula for success.

Given the fact that a protectorate of rather questionable human contrivance had replaced a regime of divine inception, and a brother-in-law of no particular pedigree was trying to fill the shoes of a regal old man, it is problematical whether under even the most favorable circumstances the new government could have controlled the furies set loose by Henry Tudor's death. To make matters worse, Edward Seymour proved to be hopelessly inadequate. Elevated by fortune to the "place of a king," it soon became apparent that the Protector did not know how to behave like a king. His initial attraction had been his avuncular relationship to a nine-year-old boy and the fact that he had been "so moderate that all thought him their own." Once in office the Duke showed that he could devise but not execute, order but not ingratiate, command but not delegate. Insensitive to others and unaware of deficiencies in himself, his behavior deteriorated into unwarranted arrogance, and his generous, if naïve, efforts to better the commonweal were distorted and vitiated by a disastrous combination of pettiness, inattention to details, and refusal to bother with the endless drudgery of effective leadership. This Duke of good intentions but little discretion wished to rule with tolerance and liberality but lacked the ruthlessness and tact to control a wolf pack of office-seeking sycophants, land-hungry colleagues and militant religious reformers. The full measure of Somerset's failure as a man and a leader became evident when his brother Thomas sought to engineer his overthrow by a combination of petticoat politics and palace intrigue which eventually ended in fratricide, and in the process nearly destroyed Elizabeth Tudor.

Thomas Seymour's refusal to bridle envy and vanity for the sake of the common good was symptomatic of the most corrosive element of the new reign. He could not abide the thought that the sheerest accident of timing had made his brother senior uncle and thus Lord Protector. He begrudged the Duke and Duchess their wealth and good fortune, and felt that he had received a mere crumb from the feast of titles and offices gobbled up by those well-beloved councillors once their master was safely buried. It was insulting that the junior uncle to a king should receive only the Barony of Sudley and the office of Lord Admiral and be denied a position in Parliament commensurate with his nearness to the Prince. With some justice Thomas argued that his brother had usurped the position of Lord Protector and that Henry had never intended that the protectorship and governorship of the King's body should be in the hands of the same person. He was scornful of his brother's inept tolerance, angered by his haughty manners and covetous of his authority, for Baron Sudley was a man "fierce of courage, courtly in fashion, in person stately, [and] in voice magnificent." It should be added, however, that he was also deemed "somewhat empty in matter," and years later Elizabeth described him as a gentleman of "very little judgment." Everywhere Thomas Seymour looked, his horizons were obscured by the presence of his lordly brother. So deliberately and wantonly he set about the Protector's destruction. That he failed was a reflection more of his own ill-conceived methods than of his brother's strength or wisdom.

One of the most awkward legacies of the previous reign was the presence of four noble ladies: Catherine Parr, the Queen Dowager; the precocious but still adolescent Lady Elizabeth; the aging and rebellious Lady Mary; and Lady Jane Grey, Henry's grandniece. All four were unmarried and therefore useful weapons in the battle for political power in a society which believed with Robert Greene "that how perfect a woman be either in virtue, beauty, or wealth, yet they are to men necessary evils." Thomas Seymour had no doubt as to how necessary they could be. From the start he cast predatory eyes on the two ladies who stood closest to the throne and suggested that he be allowed to marry royalty, but even he was sufficiently realistic to remark that "I love not to lose my life for a wife. It has been spoken of, but it cannot be." Moreover, Elizabeth was too young and Mary too obstinate to be politically rewarding. It was wiser to look elsewhere for a wife, and he opted for Catherine Parr. The two had known one another for years and there had been talk of marriage long before Catherine attracted Henry's wandering eye. Now the Dowager Queen was free to follow her fancy, and by all accounts Thomas had immense sexual magnetism. The two were secretly married within four months of the old King's death. Somerset and especially his Duchess were outraged when they learned the news, and much to the irritation of the newlyweds they took revenge by withholding Catherine's jewels on the ground that they were state property and could not be bequeathed by the late monarch.

Seymour established his bride at Sudley Castle along with two other important damsels — Elizabeth Tudor and Jane Grey. Elizabeth's presence was one of the fringe benefits of his marriage, for the Princess had been in the Dowager's charge ever since her father's death. Jane had been purchased; her father, the Marquis of Dorset, had placed his daughter in Seymour's hands for a handsome sum in the hope that the Lord Admiral might be able to arrange a marriage with the young King. Thomas "spared no cost his lady to delight or to maintain her princely royalty," and for a time every unsatisfied fortune-hunter and patron-seeker found a warm welcome at Sudley. Elizabeth, both politically and sexually, was the center of attraction. Her quiet, private existence as the King's daughter was over; she was now a princess in a political world that counted man "the agent, woman the patient," and Thomas wasted no time in demonstrating the truth of the precept. As master of Sudley he possessed keys to every room of the castle, including Elizabeth's bedroom. The dates are obscure, but before long Thomas was romping with his wife's youthful charge. Frolicking soon gave way to disporting in bed, a pinch on the buttocks, and an occasional not so innocent kiss. The Queen was unusually broad-minded but when she became pregnant and at Whitsun caught her handsome husband and stepdaughter "all alone, he having her in his arms," she ordered Elizabeth out of the house. It is senseless to speculate upon the Princess's emotional reaction to Seymour's attentions. She had reached "the fire of full fourteen" and it was an accepted biological truth that the female of the species was by nature born to "entertain and nourish voluptuousness and idleness." The burden of proof rested with the lady in question, for the Book of Proverbs was explicit on the point: "Who shall find a virtuous woman?" The answer was certainly not at Sudley Castle, and it is just as well for Elizabeth's reputation that she left when she did, for within the year Thomas was looking for another wife.

Elizabeth temporarily moved to Cheshunt, the seat of Sir Anthony Denney, and there she learned of her stepmother's delivery of a baby girl and the Queen Dowager's death a week later on September 5, 1548. As her servant and confidante Catherine Ashley eagerly pointed out, the Princess could now have Thomas Seymour if she willed so long as "my Lord Protector and the Council were pleased therein." This, of course, was the difficulty. Though she blushed at any mention of his name, Elizabeth astutely refused to see the widowed Lord Admiral, and when her Cofferer, Thomas Parry, asked whether she would consider Seymour if the Council consented, Elizabeth answered that she had no intention of telling him her mind and indignantly inquired who had put him up to such a question in the first place. Elizabeth was growing up; not only was she discovering the wisdom of discretion, but she was learning that to be a princess she must act like a princess.

It was not proper that a cofferer should discuss the subject of marriage with a king's daughter.

Elizabeth's instincts served her well. By January of 1549 Seymour was in the Tower, attainted for treason. His political sins were many and weighty. He was accused of having sought to seize control of the King's person and poison his mind against the Lord Protector. It was said that he had attempted to move "plain sedition" in Parliament; had sanctioned and profited from piracy on the high seas; had planned to marry the Princess Elizabeth without the permission of the Council; had gathered "a great multitude" at Sudley Castle to overthrow the government; and had sought to follow "the example of Richard III . . . to make himself king." During the ensuing investigation the government cast a wide net, sending Sir Robert Tyrwhit to Hatfield House to interrogate Elizabeth and ordering Catherine Ashley and Thomas Parry to the Tower where they regretted bitterly their "great folly that would either talk or speak of marriage to such as her."

Elizabeth in January of 1549 was an exceedingly adult young lady of fifteen, who, despite the danger, did not seek to lay "the burden upon others, as the use is of all those that are accused." Instead of blaming her servants or hiding behind her youth, she played down her affair with Seymour. Although a public airing of all that romping in bed with the barefooted Lord Admiral was acutely embarrassing, mercifully Seymour had never actually proposed marriage, and the gossip of servants could not be distorted into an acceptance on the part of the Princess. Disdainfully she informed the Lord Protector that she had nothing to conceal and could scarcely be expected to remember all of the details of anything so trivial. Catherine Ashley had never advised her to marry the Lord Admiral and she resented the rumors that she was pregnant and had been imprisoned in the Tower along with her servants. The least Somerset could do, she said, was to issue a proclamation silencing lewd tongues and "declaring how the tales be but lies." The best defense is a strong offense, but in her concern lest she "get the evil will of the people," Elizabeth was utilizing more than smart tactics; she was exhibiting a solicitude for appearances which was to be a central principle for the rest of her life. "Though unworthy," she was nevertheless one "of the king's majesty's sisters" and as such had a role to fulfill.

Henceforth Elizabeth was to show herself to be a master at playing a role. She set her mind to the study of those precepts which might be "useful for the government of her life" and, along with her brother, sought to adorn and furnish herself "with all the accomplishments which are fitting a prince." She determined to be "careful and cautious in all . . . deportments," keeping her "old maiden shame'fastness," for if there was one thing she had learned it was that "a spot is soon spied in our garments, a blemish quickly noted in our doings." Long before her brother's death, the Princess had become a model of political and maidenly decorum — in dress chaste and in behavior so politic that she refused to "do anything in matters that either sound or seem to be of importance without" first checking with those who spoke for the young King.

By the time Elizabeth achieved this full metamorphosis, Somerset was dead, for "the fall of one brother proved the overthrow of the other." The Protector's decision to sanction the execution of his own brother shocked Elizabeth's generation in a way that her father's blue-bearded disposal of his wives had never done; women were, of course, expendable and wives were not blood kin. The Duke was branded "a blood sucker, a murderer, a parricide," and "a ravenous wolf." Whatever else Somerset may have been he was not a "ravenous wolf," and therein lay his downfall. He had been insufficiently lupine in those areas where it really counted. His mild efforts to reestablish concord and obedience in religion had inspired no one to settle their differences or compromise their beliefs. Instead the Prayer Book of 1549 and the Act of Uniformity bred discord and debate, as radical divines clamored for further doctrinal and ceremonial reform, and Cornwall and Devonshire peasants rose in revolt demanding a return to the good old days of King Harry. Socially and economically the Lord Protector's policies were even more unsettling, and his high-minded efforts to end enclosures and tax wealthy sheep raisers produced rebellion in Norfolk so radical in its religious and social ideology that it shook Tudor society to its landowning toes. If order, priority and degree were to survive, the Lord Protector would have to step down, and his political destruction was achieved in October of 1549 by a palace revolution led by John Dudley, Earl of Warwick. A year and a half later Somerset was executed as an overly ambitious man who "sought his own glory." His death was a brutal commentary upon sixteenth-century politics: There was no defense save power itself against those in authority who feared for their own safety. Opposition by definition was disloyalty, and retirement from power was impossible in an age where economic affluence was equated to political right-thinking. Seymour could not be trusted in office or out of it, and therefore there was only one safe place for him.

The Duke of Northumberland, as Dudley soon became, was noticeably less successful than his decapitated predecessor in revitalizing the kingdom. His tenure was even less secure, for he ruled directly through a king who had been declared at twelve to be of age, and Edward was no rock on which to build a political future. His saturated little mind had been steeped in a sense of duty befitting a prince but his soul had been wrung dry of compassion as he coldly watched his uncles go to the block. A rather timid and priggish little imp was rapidly becoming a formidable Protestant Joshua whose savage precepts were that none were too old to learn and that there could be no excuse for acting contrary to God's law — dangerous commandments from a monarch whose conscience was every bit as tender as his father's and who could one day write his will in blood. As it was, Edward died, but one historical interpretation argues that it was not the ruthless and politically desperate Duke who sought to manipulate the succession and bar Mary Tudor from the throne, but the young King, who was determined to save his "chosen people of England" from the Catholic Antichrist.

Northumberland had bullied and cajoled the church into a stance far to the left of Somerset's Prayer Book of 1549. Theologically it was unabashedly Protestant; altars gave way to tables, priests became biblical teachers of God's word, the mass was transformed into a communion, and the princes of the church were stripped of their diocesan riches and turned into salaried servants of the government. It took no great feat of the imagination even on the part of a rather conventional, military-minded peer to predict what Catherine of Aragon's daughter would do to the men who had desecrated her mother's church and enriched themselves with the spoils of the ancient ecclesia. Northumberland, like the late Lord Admiral, turned to marriage as a way out of his political difficulties. He gave thought to Elizabeth as a likely bride for his son, but in the end he chose the more malleable Jane Grey, and in May of 1553 the lady was married to Guildford Dudley. The Duke was gambling on a male heir from this marriage, but before nature could run its course, Edward's health, precarious at best, began its precipitous decline. By July 5 he was dead of consumption, but before he died, the young Prince performed his final service to his church and kingdom. He sought to save the realm from the clutches of his sister Mary, and he wrote out a series of devices for the succession, the last of which willed his crown to Lady Jane and her heirs and pronounced both his sisters to be illegitimate. Reluctantly the Council backed Northumberland and the royal judges issued the necessary deed of settlement under the Great Seal. Everyone signed, and letters went out in Queen Jane's name calling upon her loyal subjects "to disturb, repel, and resist the feigned and untrue claim of the Lady Mary, bastard daughter to our great uncle, Henry VIII." Mary Tudor's reaction was a call to arms; Elizabeth's was to remain discreetly at Hatfield House despite Northumberland's best efforts to entice her to London. Wisely she would have nothing to do with the new Queen's commissioners, who offered her land and money if she would renounce her claim to the throne and acknowledge her cousin as rightful Queen. It was a desperately awkward situation: if she opted for Northumberland's gang and Mary was successful, she would be destroyed; if she joined her sister and the Duke triumphed she would also be destroyed. The Princess resolved her dilemma by appealing to a principle which she utilized throughout her life: strict legitimacy. She informed the commissioners that her sister was the only lady with whom they should do business, for as long as Mary lived she had no title to resign. She then became conveniently ill and waited upon events, which shortly proved that her father's will was still to be reckoned with; indeed, rumor reported that such had been the majesty of Henry's anger that his tomb had cracked open on the stormy night of Edward's death.

The reign of Queen Jane was over in less than a fortnight. Northumberland's army vanished; his friends slipped their collars and turned their coats; and Mary Tudor, largely because God and her father had been such close allies, was acknowledged the rightful heir to "this realm of England."

"Great is Truth and It shall prevail." Such was the opening passage of the Act of Restitution which swept history clean, erasing Henry VIII's divorce and the new Queen's bastardy. No Canute ever called with greater confidence and good will upon the tides to retreat than did Mary Tudor. There could be no doubting God's hand, for Mary had endured humiliation, sickness and disgrace for this triumphal moment on 30 July, 1553, when London welcomed her as rightful ruler of the kingdom. She owed her God a debt both of gratitude and of expiation. The declaration made seventeen years before, acknowledging her father to be Supreme Head of the Church and her mother's marriage to be incestuous, still rankled. Others had proved their faith in the face of fire and sword, but Mary had groveled before man's law, and no amount of belly wisdom about oaths extracted by fear being empty in the eyes of God could alleviate the nagging pain that in the test she had proved to be deficient. Never again would she be weak. With each passing year determination had grown. Under Edward she and her faithful servants had defiantly ridden into London displaying black crosses and rosaries, and when private mass was denied her, Mary continued to ignore the law by hiding a priest in her house and hearing mass in secret. Locked away in the melancholy of her dreams, Mary Tudor had become a recluse for whom God's majesty far outshone the luster of an earthly crown, and little thought was given to the practical politics of ever translating hope into reality. Now by the Lord's doing she was Queen — a "good, easily influenced" woman who was "inexpert in worldly matters, and a novice all round," said the new Spanish Ambassador — and she was being asked to turn back the tide and restore the comfortable, lax church of the days before her father's conscience had crept too near another lady of the court.

Everyone, including Mary, expected an inexperienced spinster queen to have a husband. Marriage during her father's and brother's life had been impossible, but now a man was needed to fulfill the biological imperative of royalty and to share the burdens of governing a kingdom rapidly sinking into heresy. The twenty-seven-year-old Edward Courtenay was the most popular candidate at court and in the country at large. He was left over from the Tudor family housecleaning that had swept the dynastic attic clear of potential heirs to the throne. Fifteen years in the Tower had improved neither his mind nor his emotional stability, but it had not tainted his Plantagenet blood. He was still Edward IV's great-grandson. Equally important, he was a Catholic. Mary, however, had set her middle-aged heart on the son of the man who almost alone had defended her mother and the Catholic cause in England. The Emperor Charles was the imperial symbol of a world Mary had lost, and to marry his son Philip was to return to an alliance between Spain and England — the diplomatic heritage which had been responsible for the Queen herself. Two deceptively mild cousins made the marriage possible; Mary who against the overwhelming advice of her Council and the wishes of her Parliament determined to "choose as God inspired her," and the Emperor who recognized the importance of an island astride his maritime lifeline between Spain and the Lowlands. "Fleshly consideration," as one Spaniard modestly phrased it, entered the decision almost not at all. For the groom it was a diplomatic and dynastic obligation; for the bride it was a spiritual panacea which would redress a generation of wrongs.

The tragedy of Mary's reign rested in a dilemma inherent in the Tudor monarchy — loyalty to the person of the sovereign as spiritual and symbolic head of the kingdom was constantly being undermined by opposition to those policies which the prince as political leader of state chose to devise and enforce. The Queen made the mistake of confusing the welcome she received as Henry Tudor's daughter with enthusiasm for Roman Catholicism, and of forgetting that the monarch could not be all things to all subjects unless somewhere among the discordant factions within the realm there was either a hard core of agreement or a broad area of indifference to royal policy. Neither condition existed in 1553. There was no accord on Mary's determination to reunite her erring land with Rome or to force it to accept her marriage to Philip, and no willingness to shrug off the Queen's policies as issues of little immediate concern best left to those in authority. The laughter of Erasmian humanism and the easygoing ways of the Renaissance papacy had long since given way to the moral indignation and stern reprisals of Paul IV on one side and the uncompromising zeal of Protestants on the other. No one as yet denied the divinity of kings, but for an increasing minority on each end of the religious spectrum divinity was becoming partisan. Neither Mary's neurotic personality nor the policies she so urgently advocated could reach into men's hearts or curb the extremists. To make matters more difficult, her Council was enlarged to unworkable and irresponsible proportions in the fond expectation that men of moderation and self-sacrifice, be they Protestant or Catholic, could infuse the Queen's leaderless kingdom with renewed purpose and vitality. The result was a cumbersome conglomerate of fifty who, one observer noted, changed "everything they have decided" and did "nothing but raise difficulties." It was not a body on which a Queen desperately in need of advice could rely, and more and more she turned to the agile tongue and deceptively dispassionate mind of Simeon Renard, the astute ambassador sent by the Emperor to arrange for the arrival and marriage of his son Philip.

Renard had a great deal of excellent counsel to offer, especially on the subject of the Queen's young sister, the central theme of which was that Elizabeth was likely to "become a great danger, unless some remedy can be found." He made no bones about the fact that his solution was the ax.

Elizabeth had moved one step closer to the crown. In doing so she had become politically even more magnetic, an irresistible attraction for every would-be traitor in search of a royal sponsor for his cause. Political charm was further heightened by something almost as dangerous: she displayed a charisma which was remarked upon from the start of the reign. "An air of dignified majesty pervades all her actions," said the Venetian Ambassador. Then he noted a fact that nearly cost Elizabeth her head in a society which could tolerate only one prince at a time: "No one can fail to suppose she is a Queen." Renard had no doubt as to the source of the danger — "The Princess Elizabeth is greatly to be feared; she has a spirit full of incantation." The Princess had a difficult role to play. As heir presumptive she was constantly in the public eye and she always responded to an audience, but as a subject "much suspected" by everyone who had something to lose by her succession, it behooved her to be retiring and self-abasing. She shared her sister's magnificent entrance into London but dressed discreetly in white, and at the Queen's coronation she carried her sovereign's train. When not in prison she tried to live within her inheritance, as the Venetian Ambassador wryly commented, so as not to awaken "the Queen's hatred and anger." The matter was a touchy one, for "there is not a lord or gentleman in the kingdom" who would not "enter her service," or place there "one of his sons or brothers"; such is "the love and affection borne her." The Ambassador was not at all convinced of the total sincerity of the Princess's behavior and added that she was forever pleading poverty, but in such a dexterous way as to incite "a tacit compassion" and therefore "greater affection." Elizabeth spent the majority of her sister's reign struggling with the elementary problem of survival, but she had the gift of twisting almost anything to her advantage. There is little wonder that Renard learned to fear her or that he thought her compliance to Mary's wish that she accept the Catholic faith was something less than frank. She had, he said, succeeded in giving "the impression that she had changed her religion" simply because she was "too clever to get herself caught."

How sincere Elizabeth was in her religious conversion is difficult to say. Protestants prefer to recount that when she went to her first mass on September 8, she "complained loudly all the way to church that her stomach ached," but we know surprisingly little about what the Princess actually believed, precisely what she had been taught as a child, or how far she had moved towards Protestantism under Edward. As Queen, Elizabeth maintained in her private chapel the pageantry and ceremony of her father's church, and whether truly or not, she told the Spanish Ambassador that she believed "God was in the sacrament of the Eucharist and only dissented from three or four things in the Mass." Whatever one makes of her words, it was certainly not difficult for a woman of twenty, reared in the doctrine of the divinity of kings and the duty of all subjects to obey a higher authority, to conform to her sister's demands. Mary still legally retained the hated title of Supreme Head of the Church of England, and no daughter of Anne Boleyn could refuse to obey that authority even when it ordered her to attend mass. Elizabeth did a certain amount of decent balking and deftly hinted that she was the victim of circumstances, endeavoring to maintain a delicate balance between compliance, which would allay her sister's suspicion that her conversion was insincere, and hesitation, which would keep the respect of the Protestant elements within the kingdom. It was a precarious pose and did not altogether work, and by early December of 1553 Elizabeth and her sister were so estranged that she left the court for Ashridge House with the Council's warning ringing in her ears — "if she refused to follow the path of duty, and persisted in concerning herself with French and heretical conspiracies, she would bitterly repent it. . . ." Conformity and the willingness to receive instruction in the Catholic faith protected the Princess against religious reprisals. Far more dangerous than the threats of her religious enemies, however, were the actions of her political friends, for before the year was out sedition was being planned on a grand scale.

Thomas Wyatt's rebellion, as the Kentish uprising of January 1554 was termed, was in its inception a four-pronged conspiracy centered in Herefordshire, Leicestershire, Devon and Kent, and scheduled for Palm Sunday, 18 March, when all four popular risings would converge on London and with French help rescue the Queen from her evil advisers and stop her Spanish marriage. What "rescuing" meant not even the rebels themselves knew, though many of them suspected it involved deposing the Queen, and there was much talk about Elizabeth and Edward Courtenay ruling jointly as man and wife. The rebels were certainly in touch with the Princess, and Renard for one was convinced that they were "trying to induce Courtenay or Elizabeth to act as their leader" but that the Princess "was too clever and sly" to be caught. And so she was; she later said that she had learned "how to keep silent" during her sister's reign, and she neither answered the rebels' letters nor left Ashridge.

What saved Mary was an accident of timing. The government wormed out of Courtenay the details of the plot before the conspirators were ready to act and before French aid had been secured. As a result Thomas Wyatt and the rest had to rush into premature treason and only the Kentish uprising exploded into armed rebellion. The rebels were in arms barely eighteen days, and by February 7 it was all over. One of the few precautionary steps taken by an otherwise almost paralyzed government was to order Elizabeth back to court where her movements could be more closely scrutinized. The Queen's letter of January 26 was ominous: "Put yourself in readiness with all convenient speed to make your repair hither to us, which we pray you, fail not to do. . . ." The Princess became too ill to oblige her sister, and it was not until February 9 that the government sent Lord William Howard, accompanied by two royal physicians, to check the truth of her complaints and to fetch her back to London. At court she was confined to her rooms while Wyatt and his fellow traitors endured their ordeal in the Tower and evidence was sought that would send Elizabeth to the block. Nothing conclusive was ever extracted from Wyatt, and at his execution on April 11 he publicly denied ever having implicated either the Princess or Courtenay. By then Elizabeth was in the Tower, dreadfully aware that she was far too dangerous to be allowed to live even if there was no clear proof of disloyalty, for two quite innocent victims of the rebellion had already been executed in February for raison d'état — Lady Jane Grey and her luckless husband Guildford Dudley.

Elizabeth entered the Tower on a rainy Sunday, March 18, the day Thomas Wyatt had planned his revolt, and her entrance is part of Gloriana's hagiography. She arrived by water at Traitors' Gate protesting her innocence and reiterating what she had already written her sister: the Tower was "a place more wonted for a false traitor than a true subject." Suddenly she sat down in the wet and refused to go farther. The Lieutenant of the Tower appealed to the one emotion guaranteed to move her — her sense of dignity. It was unbecoming to her royal status; "you had best come in, Madam, for here you sit unwholesomely." "Better sit here than in a worse place," she retorted, but rise she did and was led to her prison in the Bell Tower, where she remained for two months while the Council attempted to make up its mind what to do with a Tudor princess. The Spanish position was unequivocal: it was "indispensable to throw the Lady Elizabeth into prison, and it is considered that she will have to be executed, as while she lives it will be very difficult to make the Prince's [Philip's] entry here safe, or accomplish anything of promise." The prisoner herself expected no mercy from her sister on the grounds of kinship. It was her blood that was fatal, and as she later said in connection with her cousin of Scotland, "a kingdom knows no kindred." All she asked of Mary was that a French executioner with a sharp blade be imported to do the job.

Everyone admitted that "nothing could be proved," and with Henry VIII's daughter the fig leaf of legality had to be preserved. No one was willing to risk summary execution lest even the rumor of such an action precipitate rebellion. Moreover, there were important councillors who were determined to protect either Elizabeth or Courtenay or, what was politically more practical, both of them. Mary herself combined obstinacy with indecision. The crux of her dilemma was self-evident: the rebels would not have used her sister "unless they had more certain knowledge of her favour . . . than is yet confessed by her." Yet Elizabeth was her own blood, at least in the part that mattered. The Queen's solution was not dissimilar to Elizabeth's own when confronted years later with Mary Queen of Scots: She made no decision at all and waited upon events. Once Prince Philip arrived in England, the problem of how to handle the Lady Elizabeth could be determined within seconds in the connubial bed where, if God willed, an heir would be conceived. And so it was acrimoniously settled that the Princess should be sent to Woodstock Palace outside of Oxford under house arrest.

Elizabeth found the decision almost unbelievable, and when on May 19 she was removed from the Tower, she thought the danger to be at its height and is reported to have said: "This night I think to die." Murder was an easy way out, one which she herself would not hesitate to suggest as a convenient resolution of the problem of what to do with Mary Stuart, for the sixteenth century was perfectly aware: "It is no murder in a king to end another's life to save his own"; "if you fail, the state doth whole default, the realm is rent in twain in such a loss."

It took the Princess five days to travel to Woodstock. Try as she might to act the role of a dutiful subject, the task was well-nigh impossible. Unbidden, the guns of the Hanseatic fleet saluted her as her barge was rowed upstream to Richmond; villagers en route rang the church bells and greeted her with shouts of "God save your grace"; and Lord Williams of Thame gave a banquet in her honor to which he invited all the local gentry. Sir Henry Bedingfield, her keeper, had a difficult time with his "great lady." She was alternately proud, defiant and capricious, and her one satisfaction in the midst of infuriating restrictions at Woodstock was to be treated like royalty. When in June she fell ill with "waterish humours" and requested her sister to send the royal doctors but was told local physicians would do as well, she informed Sir Henry she would rather die than be inspected by common hands — "I am not minded to make any stranger privy to the state of my body, but commit it to God." There is no doubt that Elizabeth resented her arrest and Mary's cold dismissal of her protestations of innocence. Possibly the legend that the bitterness and futility of her life erupted into quite passable poetry scribbled in charcoal on a shutter is true:

> Oh fortune, thy wresting wavering state
>   Hath fraught with cares my troubled wit,
> Whose witness this present prison late
>   Could bear, where once was joy's loan quit.
> Thou causedst the guilty to be loosed
>   From bands where innocents were enclosed,
> And caused the guiltless to be reserved,
>   And freed those that death had well deserved
> But all herein can be nothing wrought,
>   So God send to my foes all they have thought.

It was with great relief that in April of 1555 Bedingfield learned that the event upon which the Queen had been waiting so long had finally transpired, and his prisoner could be returned to court, for Mary was pregnant. Elizabeth had been at Woodstock for just under a year, and during those months "wresting wavering" fortune had heaped more happiness upon Mary Tudor than she had known for over a generation. On July 25 she married His Royal Highness Prince Philip, Archduke of Burgundy. Four months later on November 30 came the most joyous moment of all, the day her cousin Reginald Cardinal Pole in the name of his Holiness absolved the kingdom of twenty years of schism and returned it to the papal fold. Parliament had repealed the Act of Supremacy; the Supreme Headship was no more, and the Reformation had finally been undone. No wonder the Queen was "fatter and of a better colour" than ever before. Now it appeared that part of that fatness was the child that Mary knew she carried, for she said "God will not deceive me, in Whom my chief trust is." It was not, however, entirely Mary's doing that Elizabeth was now at court. Philip, cautious prince that he was, was concerned lest his Queen die in childbirth. He believed in thinking ahead to a day when imperial interests might want to support Elizabeth against the claims of Mary of Scotland, who was about to wed the Dauphin of France. It was important to meet the girl who might yet become his wife.

God in His wisdom gave Mary Tudor neither a birth nor a death, only the unmitigated tragedy of her final years — the epithet of "bloody." Her pregnancy turned out to be ovarian dropsy; her husband, ten years her junior, could no longer force himself "to drink this cup" and in August of 1555 sailed for Flanders; and her sincerest efforts to stamp out heresy were grotesquely transformed into a holocaust. Her alliance with her good friend the Emperor led not to a revival of English influence in European affairs but to the ignominy of military defeat and the loss of Calais, the last relic of England's continental empire. Even reconciliation with Rome proved as barren as her marriage, producing only hatred and misunderstanding.

In the midst of the kingdom's troubles, the two sisters grew closer together. Elizabeth still obstinately maintained that she had been "wrongfully punished," but she was exceedingly careful not to antagonize a Queen who was becoming more and more oppressed with a sense of failure. She adroitly avoided Spanish schemes to marry her off to members of the Hapsburg tribe, largely because any marriage would have involved recognizing her as heir to the throne and this as yet Mary could not bring her Catholic soul to accept. The Princess, however, could not prevent her name from being associated with harebrained plots on the part of men who viewed her as "a liberal dame and nothing so unthankful as her sister." It was perfectly clear, at least to Simeon Renard, that "all the plots and disorders that have troubled England during the past four years have aimed at placing its government in Elizabeth's hands sooner than the course of nature would permit." Hatred of the Spanish connection, more than Catholicism, was the rallying cry of almost all who planned treason, and Mary's actions during

1556–1557 acted as salt on already inflamed wounds. What both husband and wife desired above all else was Philip's coronation as King of England, for should the Queen die, Philip's authority would cease. It was unnatural for a husband to be so inferior to his wife and dangerously impolitic to lose control of England just as the Hapsburg-Valois duel was warming up again. Philip's coronation, however, entailed disinheriting Elizabeth and setting aside Henry's will just as ruthlessly as Northumberland had attempted to do. The Queen, it was said, "may not lawfully disinherit the right heirs apparent." Ten years earlier such a statement would have been treated as nonsense, for Henry had done exactly that — he had tampered with strict legitimacy and had set aside the rightful claims of the Stuart line. Half a century later his daughter Elizabeth, stickler for legitimacy that she was, broke her father's will on this very point and rectified what she regarded as an injustice: James VI of Scotland, not one of the Suffolk breed, succeeded her on Henry's throne. Under Mary the situation was even clearer; if Lady Jane Grey had been unacceptable to the kingdom, Philip was anathema, and sedition plot after sedition plot bubbled away, fired by the desire to get rid of a Queen who "is a Spaniard at heart and loves another realm better than this."

Treason touched Elizabeth very closely. In May of 1556 Catherine Ashley, that devoted but indiscreet gossip, was back in the Tower with others of the Princess's household, and during the summer Essex men began once again to proclaim Elizabeth Queen and "her beloved bedfellow, Lord Courtenay, king." Possibly it was just as well that Courtenay died that year in exile; at least his death removed one of the uncertainties over which the Princess had no control. For herself she was faced with the impossible task of demonstrating to a deaf audience the loyalty that was written in the heart of a "true subject." In a deeply moving letter she wrote her sister in August of 1556, seeking to express in writing what lay behind words. "Oh that there were good surgeons for making anatomies of hearts, for then, I doubt not . . . that whatever others should" say out of spite "the clear light of my soul" would "glisten to the dimming of their hid malice." It is said Gloriana never made windows into men's souls; she knew the futility of it and was content with deeds. She gave men the benefit of the doubt, for who indeed can make "anatomies of hearts"? She spent a lifetime, as she said, pardoning rebels, winking at sedition and slipping over in silence "so many treasons." She was proud that she had never "bent mine ears to credit a tale that first was told me; nor was so rash to corrupt my judgment with my censure, ere I heard the cause." One of her most admirable qualities was that she rarely forgot the time when the shoe was on the other foot.

Elizabeth had said back in May of 1555 that she would be a "true subject . . . as long as life lasteth." She had not, however, specified whose life, and during the summer and fall of 1558 Mary's alloted time was running out. The Princess always remembered the spectacle of men preparing the Queen's shroud even before she was in her grave, and of power slipping away as fast as courtiers and sycophants, councillors and patron-seekers could scurry from Westminster to Hatfield House to offer her their self-interested support. The "second person" of the realm was becoming the first, and Elizabeth, recalling Northumberland's schemes to upset the legitimate succession, made plans to protect her "royal state, title and dignity" against possible Spanish designs, French intrigue on behalf of Mary Stuart, or even from the ill-starred Suffolk clan. The exact nature of the Princess's plans are only hinted at, for there was never need to implement them. In the end the Queen recognized the imperative of legitimacy, even if it meant the destruction of all that she had struggled to achieve.

During the morning of 17 November, 1558, Mary Tudor died more contentedly than she had lived, the sound of cherubim singing her way to eternal repose. Elizabeth was now a sovereign: against all reasonable expectation she had reached "the ripest fruit of all." If success is to be measured in terms of survival, she had been preeminently successful, for she had outlasted them all, and en route to her coronation she stopped to pay her respects to an allegorical figure of Time, exclaiming: "Time hath brought me hither." Time had been crucial; it had trained her, for she knew what it was "to be a subject," but it had not scarred her. Elizabeth mounted the throne with extraordinarily little bitterness for the months in the Tower and the years of mental and physical anguish which had come close to ruining her health. In the words of Sir Francis Bacon, "she did not pass suddenly from the prison to the throne with a mind embittered and swelling with the sense of misfortune. . . ." Possibly this was the true measure of her success. She had learned much and was ready to forgive and forget the eleven years between the death of her father and "hope Wednesday," the day it was learned that Mary was dying. It was now time for the last of Henry's children to fulfill the inscription: "Imitate your father . . . surpass him and none will surpass you." There was no doubt in the Spanish Ambassador's mind that she intended to do exactly that. "To great subtlety," he reported, "she adds very great vanity. She has heard great talk of her father's mode of action, and means to follow it."

FOUR

To Be a King and Wear a Crown

Partly for honour, partly for conscience, [partly] for
causes to herself known.
— *The Queen's message to Commons
delivered by Sir James Croft, 1572*

THE SIXTEENTH-CENTURY male was clinically precise in his condemnation of womankind — "light of credit, lusty of stomach,
impatient, full of words, apt to lie, flatter & weep"; their tears
"more of dissimulation than of grief"; and "desirous rather to
rule than to be ruled." As a general description of the female
of the species the quotation may lack substance, but as a list of
qualities with which Gloriana's biographers must struggle, the
statement strikes embarrassingly close to the mark. Queen Bess
indeed was singularly "full of words," "apt to lie, flatter and
weep," was a master of dissimulation, and made no bones
about her will to rule; "I will have here," she told that elegant
exponent of masculine prerogative, the Earl of Leicester, "but
one mistress and no master. . . ." To the Scottish Ambassador
she phrased it less crudely: "So long as I live, I shall be Queen
of England." From the moment there was official word of her

sister's death, Elizabeth insisted upon her royal authority, and she made the point gracefully but firmly in her first speech to a delegation from both houses of Parliament in February of 1559. It is, she said, "a very great presumption, being unfitting and altogether unmeet for you" to take upon yourselves "to draw my love to your liking or frame my will to your fantasies; for a guerdon [a reward] constrained and a gift freely given can never agree together." Seven years later the message was more bluntly put: "I will never be by violence constrained to do anything." Her father, who had once declared that he did "not choose any one to have it in his power to command me, nor will I ever suffer it," would have wholeheartedly agreed.

Years later Elizabeth was to say that when she had come to the throne, she entered "into the school of experience, bethinking myself of those things that best fitted a king — justice, temper, magnanimity, judgment." Forty-five years of experience taught her much, but the young Queen's concept of majesty in 1559 came to her ready-made. It was the product of countless generations of indoctrinated deference to authority — "To submit myself to all my governors, teachers, spiritual pastors, and masters. To order myself lowly and reverently to all my betters." Elizabeth had known what it was to be "a second person" and had accepted the unquestioning obedience required of a "true subject." Now that she was both father and governess to her kingdom, she expected no less from her own children; it was "a strange thing that the foot should direct the head," and she was sure that "no king fit for his state will suffer such absurdities."

If the sterility that pervaded so much of Mary's reign stemmed from her unbending commitment to a dead past that could be resurrected neither by prayer nor by statute, then the gods were singularly cruel, for Elizabeth was almost as anachronistic and far more parochial than her sister. Her model for "a king fit for his state" was Henry VIII — the special nature of his kingly intelligence, the majesty that resided in his royal veins, and the ruthlessness with which he protected his freedom of action and prerogative. If there was a single refrain which resounded throughout the Queen's life, it was her oft reiterated conviction that as Henry Tudor's heir she moved in a royal company which lived by standards peculiar to itself and that the quality of her royal judgment must of necessity outweigh any quantity of vulgar sentiment expressed in Parliament or Council. She had "as good a courage . . . as ever my father had" and she was the "anointed Queen."

Whatever Elizabeth may have felt about the doctrinal forms of religion, she believed without reservation in the divinity of kings. No one on November 18, 1558, doubted that God's hand had restrained "inimical fortune" and preserved Elizabeth for this moment, and whether she actually spoke the words or not, the young Queen certainly believed that "this is the Lord's doing; it is marvellous in our eyes." From the start she recognized the extent of her responsibility to God, and in 1563, when she was resolutely resisting parliamentary pressure to name her successor, she burst out: "To whom much is committed much is required. Think not that I . . . will in this matter . . . be careless. For I know that this matter toucheth me much nearer than it doth you all, who, if the worst happened, can lose but your bodies; but if I take not that convenient care that it behoveth me to have therein, I hazard to lose both body and soul."

For those who bargained with their souls in matters of state, the word of a king assumed unique importance, and Elizabeth never tired of speaking "in the word of a Prince" or referring to her "princely understanding." Not long before she came to the throne she had reminded her sister of the "old saying, that a King's word was more than another man's oath." Now that she

held the sceptre she sought, sometimes with embarrassing consequences, to apply the principle herself. She assured Parliament in 1566 that she would "never break the word of a prince,
spoken in a public place, for my honour's sake. And therefore
I say again, I will marry. . . ." As the critics said, women were
by nature "light of credit," and she wisely added the saving
codicil "as soon as I can conveniently." Two years later she was
less circumspect with Mary of Scotland, and informed her
cousin "on the word of a prince" that nothing would ever
move her "to ask anything of you which may endanger you or
touch your honour." Elizabeth had much to learn about a
prince's word and the art of kingly government, and her royal
promise to Mary Stuart was to become a source of endless dis-
agreement between the Queen and her Council, but in her
handling of the affairs of state, Gloriana remained rigidly consistent — she would listen to advice "and thereupon make
choice of what she should think meetest for her honour." Her
father had once informed James V of Scotland that "there is
nothing, after the glory of Almighty God, in this world so
much to be rendered by kings, princes or any honest persons,
or so highly to be regarded and defended, as their honour,
estimation, good fame and name. . . ." The good fame of
kings, however, was not for inferiors to decide, and Elizabeth
made the point clear to a delegation of Dutch burghers:
queenly promises were not always to be taken literally, for
princes "transact business in a princely way and with a
princely understanding such as private persons cannot have."

The sacred honor of a sovereign was not simply a matter of
the prerogatives of office which were embodied in Gloriana's
marvelous retort to Sir Robert Cecil when he told her that she
must go to bed — "little man, little man, the word *must* is not
to be used to princes." Nor did it involve the freedom so essential to monarchy mentioned by Sir Francis Knollys when he

told Commons that the order to execute Mary Stuart would "be more honourable to her Majesty if the doing thereof came of her free mind without our motion." Instead, it had to do with the quality of kingship itself, that divinely inspired knowledge that led Henry VIII to exclaim that he "had been directed in the mean way of truth, and therefore was meet to be arbiter between the others to reduce them to the truth," and Elizabeth to announce in a message to Parliament that "her Majesty is fully resolved, by her own reading and princely judgment, upon the truth of the Reformation which we have already. . . ." The Queen, like her father, fancied herself a theological expert and assured Commons that her judgment had been confirmed "by the letters and writings of the most famous men in Christendom," but ultimately she took her stand less on the quantity of her knowledge than on the quality, for "if I were not persuaded that mine were the true way of God's will, God forbid I should live to prescribe it to you."

Elizabeth belonged by birth to a highly exclusive royal club, and she did not hesitate to inform the Polish Ambassador in July of 1597 that it was not sufficient to be elected. She had been a member for forty years, and in brilliant extemporaneous Latin she told the unfortunate man that the only excuse she could find for his sovereign's disgraceful behavior was "his being a King, not of many years — and that not by right of blood, but by right of election. . . ." Blood counted. Henrician England took seriously the sedition of Mr. Edward Foster, who had impiously questioned "if the King's blood and his were both in a dish or saucer what difference were between them and how should a man know the one from the other." Elizabeth had her father's blood, and in 1582 she was deeply shocked that a commission of Dutch merchants should have dared to approach her "fiancé," the Duke of Alençon, as an equal: "You shoemakers, carpenters and heretics, how dare you speak in such terms to a man of royal blood like the Duke of Alençon. I would have you know that when you approach him or me, you are in the presence of the two greatest princes in Christendom." The diplomatic rhetoric and exaggeration are transparent, but so also is the defense of her royal species. When Philip II of Spain died, it was not the Queen's magnanimity and religious tolerance that persuaded her to consign his soul to heaven; whatever might have been their disagreements on earth, Philip as a "potent prince" and God's deputy in this world had a right to claim a very special place in the next. With Catherine de' Medici Elizabeth was far less considerate, but then the Queen Mother of France was not of royal birth: she was descended from a long line of Italian moneylenders. When Elizabeth's secretary wrote Catherine complimenting her by referring to "two Queens from whom, though women, no less was expected in administration of affairs and in the virtue and arts of government than from the greatest men," Gloriana ordered the offending sentence to be struck out. "The arts and principles which she employed in governing," she said, "were of a far other sort than those of the Queen Mother." Indeed they were; they were divinely inspired, and Elizabeth did not like invidious comparisons to common people, especially women. It took almost a decade, and there were a host of motives at work, but in the end Bess found it impossible to marry Robert Dudley, the only man she ever came close to loving, because "the aspiration to greatness and honour which is in me could not suffer him as a companion and a husband."

Elizabeth took the divinity of kingship seriously; even in the teeth of the evidence it was necessary not only to believe the word of a prince but also to assume his good intentions. If "the name of king" was "to be sacred" then care had to be taken "lest any stigma be cast upon this name by others"; and the prescription had to begin at home. Ministers might err but never kings, and Elizabeth did not hesitate to place the burden of guilt squarely where God had ordained it: on evil councillors. In December of 1559 she asked the Catholic prelates of her late sister's church to "recollect; was it our sister's conscience made her so averse to our father's and brother's actions, as to undo what they had perfected? Or was it not you, or such like advisers, that dissuaded her, and stirred her up against us . . . ?" The same double standard applied to rebels, and she informed Mary Stuart's seditious subjects that though their sovereign "were guilty of all they charged her with, I cannot assist them while their Queen is imprisoned." To Mary herself she wrote she could not allow her cousin "being by God's ordinance the prince and sovereign, to be in subjection to them that by virtue and law are subjected to her."

When Elizabeth told the Scottish Ambassador that as long as she lived she would be Queen of England, she added an important sentence: "When I am dead they shall succeed me that have the most right." Legitimacy was the crux of the matter and Gloriana was inordinately touchy on the subject, both as a general principle and as a question of personal survival. She was willing to risk confrontation with her Parliament in her determination to defend her cousin of Scotland's legitimate rights as heir presumptive to the Tudor throne, and she was even willing to overthrow her father's will in order to maintain that right. Edward and Mary had been ready to contemplate setting aside the legitimate blood succession because they could appeal to a higher authority, but for Elizabeth it was as if belief in legitimacy — her own as well as others — was a substitute for religion. Within months of her succession she hotly upbraided her commissioners at the Anglo-French peace talks of Cateau-Cambrésis for permitting the French delegates to discuss her claim to her father's throne as if it were open to doubt, and she curtly told them that she would never "permit any over whom we have rule" to "make doubt, question, or treaty of this matter." Eight years later her conversation with the Spanish Ambassador was undoubtedly calculated, when she told him that if any of her Council ever dared to advise her to aid another prince's rebellious subjects "she would hang him as a traitor," but when Henry IV of France was confronted with an overmighty and treasonous subject, her advice came from the heart: "In such cases there is no middle course; we must lay aside clemency and adopt extreme measures."

Although Elizabeth liked to tout the fact that she had spent a lifetime winking at treason, in a crisis she could be almost as bloodthirsty as her father. She wept, but in the end she signed the death warrants of both Mary of Scotland and Thomas Howard, Duke of Norfolk, and her treatment of her own kind, especially if they were "very near us in blood" was in the customary Tudor tradition. The Queen saw to it that the Suffolk sisters of Lady Jane Grey spent most of their adult lives in the Tower or under house arrest. The same instinct for self-preservation operated in the winter of 1569–1570, after the abortive rebellion of the Northern earls. Elizabeth "by her special commandment" reversed the instructions of the Earl of Sussex to "execute some for example" but to "extend her Majesty's mercy to the serving men of meaner sort"; instead, the rich were allowed to appease the Queen's wrath with gold while 750 of the poor paid with their lives, their bodies ordered "to remain till they fall to pieces where they hang." When Anthony Babington and his fellow traitors were caught plotting the assassination of the Queen in 1585, Elizabeth thought no death too barbarous for attempted regicide and demanded that "the manner of their death, for more terror, be referred to her Majesty and her Council." Not even William Cecil's assurance that the customary hanging, castration and disembowelment could be protracted by a skilled executioner into a death as "terrible as any other new device" satisfied a woman whose father, fifty years before, had ordered "such dreadful execution to be done" upon the unfortunate remnants of the Yorkshire rebels "as they may be a fearful spectacle to all others hereafter that would practice any like matter."

The doctrines of dynastic legitimacy and the divinity of kings may have been psychologically necessary to a young woman whose position in the order of inheritance was her single redeeming feature in the eyes of a European community which viewed her sex, the circumstances of her birth and her religion as crippling handicaps, but they also fettered her to a rapidly receding past. They produced an approach to domestic and international affairs that was dangerously inflexible and archaic, and made the Queen an uncompromising exponent of the status quo. As Francis Bacon said, "Her Majesty loveth peace; next she loveth not change." From the moment she succeeded to the throne, Elizabeth was at odds with her Council and her Parliament on almost every important national issue, largely because her orientation was to the past, not to the future. Her perspective was parochial, never visionary; and "her wisest men and best counsellors were often sore troubled to know her will in matters of state, so covertly did she pass her judgment." This indeed was the quality that drove the Queen's long-suffering ministers to distraction — she was such an artist at dissimulation, so "full of words" and so "apt to lie" that it was almost impossible to know exactly what she intended. But through the verbal smokescreen a single theme was always discernible: her style of ruling, her policy and her majesty were all intensely personal and essentially selfish.

Early in the reign it was caustically noted by a jaundiced Protestant that the Queen was "entirely given over to love, hunting, hawking and dancing, consuming day and night with trifles. . . . He who invents most ways of wasting time is regarded as one worthy of honour." Despite the Puritan exaggeration, the picture contains an element of truth. God had given Elizabeth her throne, and like Pope Leo X she had every intention of enjoying it. Unlike her brother and sister she was content solely to satisfy herself, and nothing flattered her ego as much as the love of her subjects.

Love was the Queen's favorite and most overworked word, and historians, hypnotized by her dulcet phrases, have never wearied of extolling that inspired romance which "mere English" Bess carried on with her loutish, wayward people. Yet the love she demanded was very special; it was the devotion offered a goddess, not a woman, and it was largely one-sided. "Your love for me," she told Oxford undergraduates in 1592, "is of such kind as has never been known or heard of in the memory of man. Love of this nature is not possessed by parents; it happens not among friends, no, not even among lovers, whose fortune does not always include fidelity as experience teaches. It is such a love as neither persuasion, nor threats, nor curses can destroy. Time has no power over it. Time, which eats away iron and wears away the rocks cannot sever this love of yours. It is of this your services consist, and they are of such kind that I would think they would be eternal, if only I were to be eternal." The words are matchless but so is the egotism. Love for Gloriana was service, sacrifice and adulation. She loved her people as an actress loves her followers, their applause, their envy, and the knowledge that she can control them by artistry. But she never allowed herself to be enslaved by her worshipers, for the essence of her divinity and therefore of her power was freedom. Elizabeth invariably demanded more than she gave.

When a girl of twenty-four, who had been on the throne less than a year, lashed out at her councillors for their failure to quash any discussion, no matter how theoretical, that suggested she might not be the rightful queen of England, or when she could whip herself into a fury over the thought of Mary Stuart delighting in an "unjust and dishonourable usurpation of the arms, style and title" of her kingdom, considerably more than an academic adherence to the principles of legitimacy and divinity was involved. Elizabeth may have consciously modeled her royal stance upon the immense Holbein icon of ancestral worship and legitimacy which dominated her privy chamber at Whitehall Palace, with its five-foot ten-inch image of her father who had kept "his subjects from the highest to the lowest in due obedience," but for all her talk, she knew herself to be closer to the Duke of Somerset than to Henry Tudor. As a woman she could not hope to be a complete king. Sir William Paget had told the Lord Protector that he was now in the "place of a king," so "then, sir, for a king do like a king." The unhappy Duke had found the advice more easily voiced than followed, for he lacked the essential ingredient of kingship: legitimacy. Elizabeth was also deficient: her sex was inadequate for her office, and she went through life compensating and apologizing. It was difficult to do otherwise, for Tudor England knew that "every woman would willingly be a man, as every deformed wretch, a goodly and fair creature; and every idiot and fool, learned and wise." Her femininity was persistently flung in her face. Her parents had made no effort to conceal their disappointment in her sex, and her educators had commented that "the constitution of her mind is exempt from female weakness and she is endued with a masculine power of application." After the defeat of the Armada Pope Sixtus V could not but admire a ruler who was "only a woman," and no self-respecting male could understand how Tudor England "could be swayed and controlled at the beck of a woman." Even in death Gloriana was reminded of the fact that she had not been born a man: Her tomb bears the inscription: "adorned with excellent adornments both of body and mind, and excellent for princely virtues beyond her sex." Elizabeth stood in the "place of a king" and the challenge was to prove that nature had not framed man's "body to superiority and set the print of government in his face." If one could paint Gloriana as she sat for forty-five years beneath the image of her father's majestic masculinity, the portrait would surely reveal a cruel amalgam of insecurity, overcompensation, father worship and sexual ambivalence. Over and over she spoke of her sex, sometimes with bravado, sometimes as excuse, sometimes in apology. In 1554, when she was conducted into the Tower with a demoralizing display of armed force, she wanted to know whether it was really necessary "for me, being alas but a weak woman." Nine years later, in one of her earliest confrontations with Parliament over the succession, she neatly balanced the inadequacies of her sex with the superior quality of her majesty: "The weight and greatness of this matter might cause in me, being a woman wanting both wit and memory, some fear to speak and bashfulness besides, a thing appropriate to my sex. But yet, the princely seat and kingly throne wherein God . . . hath constituted me, maketh these two causes to seem little in mine eyes. . . ." By the year of the Armada, Elizabeth was no longer admitting to God that she was "by kind a weak woman," without "sufficient ability to rule these Thy kingdoms of England and Ireland." Now she proudly told her troops at Tilbury: "I know I have but the body of a weak and feeble woman; but I have the heart and stomach of a King and of a King of England too." By 1601, the year of her "golden speech" to Parliament, her phraseology was almost entirely masculine when she spoke of her "kingly dignity," "title of a king," and "glorious name of a king." The language of royalty was, of course, male, but with every passing decade, Elizabeth became, as Robert Cecil enigmatically put it, "more than a man and, in truth, something less than a woman."

Elizabeth's sex was an embarrassment, but it was all she had to work with, and the Queen could be devastatingly feminine. It was to be expected that a woman should spend "a good part of the day tricking and trimming, pricking and prinning, prancking and pouncing, girding and lacing, and braving up themselves in most exquisite manner." Gloriana was no exception. She bedecked herself in a "bushel of pearls" and wrapped herself in the extravagant ritual befitting her sex. She could not fall back upon male superiority as the source of her authority. Unlike her father, she could never refer to herself as "the old man" to justify her actions, and she had no intention of ever being called "the old lady." The stylized pantomime of courtship in which young gallants enveloped their Juno was romantic grist to Gloriana's make-believe, but very early in her reign she warned her beardless boys that she would have no one "think my simplicity such as I cannot make distinctions among you." She was willing to risk her life to maintain a style of monarchy which she felt suitable to her femininity, and she was not above boasting that she had borne treason with a better mind "than is common to my sex — yea, with a better heart perhaps than is in some men." Even as a woman, she could not entirely escape her father. If he could not be her model, then at least he could be her opposite, and again and again she warned that "if this had been in our father's time . . . you may soon conceive how it would have been taken." But "our moderate reign and government can be contented to bear this. . . ." Perhaps she could not surpass her father as a king but just possibly she could as a queen.

How did she manage it, the extraordinary hold which was so

different from her father's majesty yet so effective? No matter how she thwarted them, scolded and insulted them — soldier and mariner, minister and parliamentarian, Catholic and Protestant, lord and commoner — they all obeyed her and offered themselves in an ecstasy of love and sacrifice. "It makes my heart leap for joy," exclaimed that blunt gospeler George Ireland, "to think we have such a jewel. It makes all my joints to tremble for fear when I consider the loss of such a jewel." The magic even captured the elderly heart of William Cecil who, after being described by his irate mistress as "old and doting," gravely replied that indeed he was ancient "and would gladly therefore retire to a church where he might pray for her." Old Cecil may have presented her with his prayers, but the venerable Bishop Aylmer, though he "had not many teeth to spare," offered her the few he had to persuade his reluctant sovereign that tooth pulling need not be painful, and Puritan John Stubbs sacrificed his right hand to the Queen's feminine dignity. He had libelously suggested that the Duke of Alençon was "unmanlike, unprince-like," un-English and was interested in an elderly English heiress solely because of the size of her royal patrimony. Elizabeth was hurt in her prerogative and her womanhood, and she permitted the ferocious punishment for slander to go through. As his right hand was struck off, loyal Mr. Stubbs "took off his hat with the left and cried aloud "God save the Queen." Gloriana's worshipers on occasion could be exceedingly irritating, but the results were well worth the annoyance when it could be said that "the Queen was never profuse in delivering out her treasure, but paid many and most of her servants part in money and the rest with grace, which as the case stood, was taken for good payment."

In her handling of John Stubbs, Elizabeth was at her savage worst, and the documents are laden with unpleasant evidence of her vanity, sarcasm, deceit, ingratitude, parsimony, pride and evil temper. She considered it within her prerogative as a queen and an expert in theology to publicly scold, correct, interrupt and chastise her divines — "To your text, Mr. Preacher"; "Do not talk about that!" "Leave that; it has nothing to do with your subject and the matter is now threadbare." And such was the royal ingratitude that she quite forgot Bishop Aylmer's dental sacrifices when in a sermon before the Queen he touched "on the vanity of decking the body too finely." Gloriana was not pleased, and she turned to her maids-in-waiting, caustically remarking that if the tactless cleric continued longer in the same vein, "she would fit him for Heaven — but he would walk thither without a staff and leave his mantle behind him."

Laymen fared no better. She informed Leicester that the hand which had made him could "beat him to the dust"; she threatened to teach Essex "better manners"; and she dismissed the House of Lords as "a collection of brains so light." In a rage she flung her slippers at Walsingham, and when an unfortunate courtier paraded before her in a frivolous cloak which she thought in poor taste, she spat on the cloth and announced that "the fool's wit has gone to rags." She rewarded her ministers with temper tantrums and irrational tirades, and drove her councillors to distraction by her procrastinations, prevarications and pettiness. Her niggardliness was legendary: throughout the reign new titles of nobility were limited to eighteen, only two of which were given to new families, and talk of six earldoms after the triumph of the Armada was quickly dropped when the Queen had second thoughts about the cost. She delighted in showing off her wit and knowledge, was constantly reminding people of her favors and was forever fishing for compliments. Early in the reign she quizzed Sir

James Melville, the Scottish Ambassador, about her rival's accomplishments. Did Mary Stuart have finer hair or a fairer complexion? who played better on the virginal? and who was the best linguist? The embarrassed Ambassador did his best and diplomatically answered that Elizabeth was "the fairest Queen in England and mine the fairest Queen in Scotland." Still not satisfied, Gloriana wanted to know who was the taller, and Sir James replied Mary was. Then in a burst of *Alice in Wonderland* logic, Elizabeth rejoined, then "she is too high, for I myself am neither too high nor too low." After the brilliant extemporaneous thrashing in Latin which she had delivered to the Polish Ambassador in July of 1597, Elizabeth complacently remarked, "I have been enforced this day to scour up my old Latin that hath lain long in rusting," and wished Essex had been there to hear her. During the last year of her life she was still at it, and after scolding the Venetian Ambassador for the Doge's failure to offer diplomatic recognition until the forty-fifth year of her reign, she concluded, "I do not know if I have spoken Italian well, still I think so, for I learnt it when a child and believe I have not forgotten it."

How did she do it? How did she end as she began with her subjects' love? It is easy to dismiss the mystery and say Englishmen had no choice; they had to make do with Elizabeth because fate had left them only a capricious idol before whom to bend the knee. Had Gloriana not existed, it would have been necessary to create her in a beleaguered kingdom desperate for a human symbol of spiritual and political unity, conditioned to believe that God spoke directly through kings, and instinctively aware that the natural leaders of a hierarchic structure could exercise authority over inferiors only if they themselves were obedient to a higher power. It was an axiom of sixteenth-century political life that "fear of some divine and supreme power keeps men in obedience," and Tudor society was fully aware that there was a secret mystery in "the pompous pride of state and dignity." Atavistic fear of the divinity that encased the throne with the aura of God's special protection and the potent memory of Henry VIII's majesty restrained the hand of William Parry, who had determined to assassinate the Queen but "was so daunted with the majesty of her presence" in which he perceived the image of her father "that his heart would not suffer his hand to execute that which he had resolved." Fear that paralyzed the hand and state pageantry that befuddled the eye are, however, insufficient explanations of what was in essence a "mystical phenomenon." The true subject did not need the gruesome spectacle of disembowelment or the church's fervent assurance of a warm welcome in hell to propel him along the path of obedience. Gloriana's safety lay neither in the sword nor in elaborate, outward obeisance but in the love and loyalty that wished her well with "heart and mind."

Obedience is a two-way proposition — the willingness to accept orders and the confidence that they will be carried out — and effective power requires careful mental conditioning on the part of both the giver and the receiver. Fortunately for Elizabeth her subjects in 1558 shared their Queen's lofty view of her high office, and though they grumbled and complained like restless and aggrieved schoolchildren, they accepted the scolding of their royal nanny as part of the natural order of things. Subjects saw her as she so often saw herself — "She is our God in earth. If there be perfection in flesh and blood, undoubtedly it is in her Majesty." The conditional nature of the eulogy was necessary to a society as sensible of the realities of human imperfection as it was hierarchical in its thinking. Sir Francis Knollys, on the other hand, good Puritan though he was, attached no strings to his acceptance of his Queen's prerogative: what "secret cause or scruple there may be in the hearts of princes, it is not for all people to know"; and William Cecil in terms both touching and convincing expressed the creed of unswerving obedience that a servant owed his master: "As long as I may be allowed to give advice, I will not change my opinion by affirming the contrary, for that were to offend God, to whom I am sworn first; but as a servant I will obey her Majesty's commandment . . . presuming that she being God's chief minister here, it shall be God's will to have her commandments obeyed . . . and shall in my heart wish her commandments to have such good success as I am sure she intendeth. . . ."

Absolute confidence in an idol who had, after all, alarming human characteristics was made more palatable by that political principle which was in part mental reflex and in part deliberate conspiracy: the myth of the evil adviser. Critics of the crown's policies and victims of the Queen's less pleasant personal qualities were afforded an outlet for their anger and frustration. In 1587 Essex was confronted with overwhelming evidence of Gloriana's vindictive pettiness. The Earl's sister, Dorothy Devereux, had married without royal or parental consent. When the Queen arrived on progress at the residence of the Earl of Warwick she discovered that Dorothy was also a guest, and promptly ordered her to be confined to her room. It was done for spite and to enrage Essex, for Elizabeth had been forewarned by Essex himself of his sister's presence and could easily have avoided an embarrassing confrontation. The Earl was furious at what he rightly construed to be a public slight to his family honor, but his handling of the affair is sociologically significant. Instead of accusing Elizabeth of outright nastiness and provocation, he jumped to the conclusion that his archrival at court, Sir Walter Raleigh, had poisoned the Queen's mind, toyed with her womanly affection and persuaded her to insult him "in the eyes of the world."

Elizabeth's reputation remained intact, but the creed that a monarch could do no wrong had its price; to sustain the myth, royalty on occasion had to be turned into a sponge of incompetence, continually absorbing sinister advice. The legend of Henry VIII's Bacchanalian revelry stemmed in part from the need to explain and justify evil actions, and with considerable political acumen but little historic justice, the Vicar of Eastbourne exempted his sovereign from all responsibility for the new religious policies of his reign on the grounds that "they that rule about the King make him great banquets and give him sweet wines and make him drunk, and then they bring him bills and he putteth his sign to them." Under Elizabeth there were no grounds for blaming that devil drink; nor was there need: she was a woman and by definition weak, frail, impatient, feeble and "void of the spirit of council." She was, as the Spanish Ambassador not very tactfully put it, "only a passionate, ill-advised woman." Although Elizabeth enjoyed the imputation of incompetence no more than her father had, there were compensations for being "a virgin prince." She was able to indulge her desire to be hateful without tarnishing her public image. "Her sex," remarked one of the less sympathetic observers of the court, "did bear out many impertinences in her words and actions. . . ."

If the fiction of royalty's perfection was to be made a political reality it was essential to divorce the crown from the uglier aspects of power. Kings were the fountain of every man's expectations and they could not be found denying a patron-seeker, refusing a pardon, making a wrong decision or levying a burdensome tax. There must always be a scapegoat to absorb the filth of partisan politics, and by Elizabeth's reign the function of a second, political king was clearly understood in practice if not in theory. William Cecil was accused of operating a *regnum Cecilianum*, but the Queen's great minister dis-

missed the title as malicious mockery and ruefully explained
the true nature of his rule. "True it is," he lamented, "that her
Majesty throweth upon me a burden to deal in all ungrateful
actions — to give answers unpleasant to suitors that miss. . . .
My burden also is this that in all suits for lands, leases and
such things, her Majesty commands me to certify the state
thereof. . . . And if the party obtain [the grant], I am not
thanked; if not, the fault (though falsely) is imputed to me."
Elizabeth took every advantage of the system. As Sir John
Harington said, "She did most cunningly commit the good
issue to her own honour and understanding; but when aught
fell out contrary to her will and intent, the Council were in
great straits to defend their own acting and not blemish the
Queen's good judgment." In desperation Cecil wrote to Walsingham in November of 1588 that "all irresolutions and lacks
are thrown upon us two. The wrong is intolerable." The system
may have been personally unjust but it was politically necessary, and Cecil sadly acknowledged that the world would always blame the "lacks and errors to some of us that are
accounted inward Councillors, where indeed the fault is not,"
but "they must be so suffered and imputed for saving the
honour of the highest."

Had Elizabeth been content to rely solely on political utility
and social instinct to achieve obedience she would have been
no better off than her sister, who suffered scurrilous attacks
upon her good name and endemic rebellion against her authority. Ultimately it was Gloriana's style that made the difference. "For a king do like a king"; like her father, Elizabeth
Tudor was a master of the art of kingship in an era that
asserted with Raleigh that "style is the man." The most difficult
problem of the age was how to reconcile total conformity with
belief in individual worth and freedom. The poets of Elizabeth's century trumpeted the authority of kings who "wear a

crown enchas'd with pearl and gold, whose virtues carry with it life and death," who "ask and have, command and be obeyed," but the heroes of her court were heedless Lucifers, men who lived by the creed that "a man must risk for a prince life, but not honour." The object of the Queen's rule was to achieve obedience without servility, service without compulsion, and conformity without degradation; what Robert Cecil referred to when he said "Her Majesty will never accept anything that is given her unwillingly," and the Queen herself meant when she announced to her loyal Commons that she had never "been willing to draw from you but what you should contentedly give."

The miracle was performed by the art of illusion, the manipulation of appearances. Subjects, in carefully staged theatricals, sought to influence the Queen without presuming to instruct — "to counsel and to admonish, gravely not grievously, sincerely not sourly" — and Gloriana was "playwright, director and leading performer." The court, as Raleigh noted, was "the great theatre" of the kingdom, and every courtier knew that it was necessary to perform well, for they had read their Seneca: "It is with life as it is with a play — it matters not how long the action is spun out, but how good the acting is." From the start Elizabeth Tudor realized her essential role: "We Princes are set as it were upon stages in the sight and view of the world." "She is," said the French Ambassador, "a prince who can act any part she pleases."

As an actress who could turn a smile into "pure sunshine," a gesture into "princely demeanour," and a glance into a "majestic look," Elizabeth was possessed of "grace" — the Spanish Ambassador preferred to say she was "possessed by the devil." Whether devilish or divine, Elizabeth enjoyed a talent for stylistic legerdemain that endowed every word and movement with effortless ease and beauty and made the most

rehearsed and artificial performance appear fresh and sponta-
neous. Philip Sidney recorded the impact of Eliza's "grace"
when he rhymed:

> When she imparts her thoughts, her words have force
> And sense and wisdom flow in sweet discourse.

Sir John Hayward recognized the same quality when he described Elizabeth's spectacular performance at her coronation:
"If ever any person had either the gift or the style to win the
hearts of people, it was their Queen. All her faculties were in
motion and every motion seemed well guided action: her eye
was set upon one, her ear listened to another, her judgment
ran upon a third, to a fourth she addressed her speech; her
spirit seemed to be every-where and yet so entire in herself, as
it seemed to be nowhere else."

If Elizabeth was the prima donna in a theatrical performance, her script was a constant reminder that "princes with
their Majesty may be oft envied and hated; without it they are
always scorned and condemned." The entire production —
lighting, props, lines, cast and even censorship — were directed
to a single dramatic end: the illusion of majesty by which to
captivate an entire kingdom. The script had been her father's,
but it was, in fact, as old as kingship itself, for playwright and
actor, stage manager and audience knew that successful majesty
involved three simple rules — never appear ridiculous by step-
ping out of character, never lose control over those closest to
the seat of power, and never destroy the hope of gain in those
upon whom you must depend. There was no need for Elizabeth to be told Roger Edwards's admonition to remember "in
all your doings . . . the majesty of your person, wherein consisteth the politique life of your people," for no aspect of the
Queen's performance is better documented than her unerring

dramatic instinct for displaying her majesty: she was "of such
state in her carriage, as every motion of her seemed to bear
majesty." Of all the descriptions of Elizabeth at her dramatic
and majestic best, the most arresting was the treasured memory
of old Bishop Godfrey Goodman, recalling the sight of his
aging Queen leaving the council chamber. It was a winter's
evening, and "show and pageants are ever best seen by torch-
light." Word had gotten out "if you will see the Queen you
must come quickly," and she was greeted by a swarm of worshipers who shouted "God save your Majesty." Elizabeth re-
acted like an old trooper, and, asking God's blessings upon her
good people, she spoke lines that she had used over and over
but never permitted to become hackneyed: "Ye may well have
a greater Prince, but ye shall never have a more loving Prince."
The words, the timing, the "grace" all had the desired effect.
"This wrought," recalled the Bishop, "such an impression upon
us . . . that all the way long we did nothing but talk of what
an admirable Queen she was, and how we would adventure our
lives to do her service."

Elizabeth spoke obsessively of love — her love for her subjects, and their "hearts and true allegiance" which were "the
greatest riches" of her kingdom — but she also knew "how to
humble the haughty spirit." In the first year of her reign the
Spanish Ambassador noted that she was "incomparably more
feared than her sister, and gives her orders and has her way as
absolutely as her father did." Her wit, her knowledge, and
above all her command of words were the weapons which
brought her haughty children to heel. She could stop Raleigh
with a line, and when in one of those rhyming contests so
beloved by Elizabethans, Sir Walter sighed:

> Though fortune conquer thee;
> No fortune base nor frail shall alter me;

Gloriana neatly deflated his ego by replying:

> Ah silly pugge wert thou so sore afraid,
> Mourn not (my Wat) nor be thou so dismaid.

In a less well authenticated encounter Raleigh scribbled on a windowpane: "Fain would I climb, yet fear I to fall"; and the Queen promptly added: "If thy heart fails thee, climb not at all." She ordered the old Welsh soldier, Sir Roger Williams, from her sight with the doubtlessly accurate comment — "Fah, Williams, pray begone: thy boots stink"; and during her coronation she dismissed the prelate who sought to anoint her with holy oil with the remark that his ointment stank. When the French Ambassador complimented her on her linguistic abilities, she would have none of his French flattery and replied "that there was no marvel in a woman learning to speak, but there would be in teaching her to hold her tongue." Indeed, as John Harington said, "when she smiled it was a pure sunshine, but anon came a storm from a sudden gathering of clouds, and the thunder fell in wondrous manner on all alike."

Wit could delight or it could devastate, but it could not awe. It was the Queen's knowledge and memory that won respect from even the most vigorous exponents of male superiority: "I know not how she penetrates everything"; "She is ignorant of nothing"; "She is of a curious and perspicacious mind, deep and prudent so that she learns from one sentence and word many and various things. . . ." Ministers might complain of her nagging interference, her delays and prevarications, but William Cecil himself confessed she was "the wisest woman that ever was; for she understood the interests and dispositions of all the princes in her time, and was so perfect in the knowledge of her own realm, that no counsellor could tell her anything she did not know before." Few sovereigns ever worked harder at their task; few princes had a better right to exclaim: "To be a King and wear a crown is a thing more glorious to them that see it, than it is pleasant to them that bear it." It was not simply the drudgery of office — the endless ritual and tireless scrutiny of detail whereby she could inform Henry IV of France that he owed her precisely £401,734/16s/5½p — but the hours that went into producing the apparently effortless rhetoric that transformed autocracy into majesty and wrapped it in a mantle of mystification so rich and colorful that no one could say exactly what she meant but everybody agreed it was worth listening to. Elizabeth's mastery of words is almost without equal in political annals: her "sexly weakness," her contentment "to be a taper of true virgin wax" to "light and comfort" her people, and her disarming request to Parliament "to accept my thankfulness, excuse my doubtfulness and take in good part my answer-answerless." No one could enthrall the "captious ears" of her subjects with contrived brilliance better than Gloriana. Her public speeches, though posing as sudden, extemporaneous outbursts of pleasure or anger, were in fact carefully rehearsed, the results of endless deletion, insertion and stylistic amendment. Early drafts were filled with satirical digs, pent-up fury and impolitic outbursts, but later editions were toned down, tactful yet forceful and always poignant. In 1566, preparing to scold a delegation of both Houses for their presumptuousness in seeking to command a queen, she wrote "I marvel not much that bridleless colts do not know their rider's hand, whom bit of kingly rein did never snaffle yet," but by the time she actually addressed her errant subjects the words had been softened to "those unbridled persons whose mouth was never snaffled by the rider, did rashly ride into it in the Common House, a public place."

Tact and timing were the carefully chosen handmaidens of

her majesty and she gave great thought to both, rarely wasting or overusing words. Unerringly she knew when to command, when to retreat, when to delay and above all when to pluck the strings of men's expectations. She knew the wisdom of ignoring human frailty, of winking at treason and keeping the knowledge of evil to herself, because she recognized that hope is the only sure antidote to sedition and that only desperation and fear of revelation will drive ambitious men to outright rebellion. Almost her first public address, announcing the membership of her Council, was a masterpiece of political poise, striking the exact balance between historical principles and expediency, asking for help yet imposing authority, flattering every man's expectations and holding even those she passed over with words of affection. "And they which I shall not appoint, let them not think the same for any disability in them but that for I do consider a multitude doth make rather discord and confusion than good counsel and of my good will you shall not doubt, using yourselves as appertaineth to good and faithful subjects." Years later John Clapham spoke of the same talent: "She suffered not at any time any suitor to depart discontented from her; and, though ofttimes he obtained not that he desired, yet he held himself satisfied with her manner of speech, which gave hope of success in a second attempt."

No one knew how to manipulate the heart as did the Virgin Queen. After scolding Leicester for his disobedience she won him back with honeyed phrases which were irresistible. "I am afraid you will suppose by my wandering writings that a midsummer moon hath taken large possession of my brains this month, but you must needs take things as they come into my head, though order be left behind me." When Cecil was dispirited with his Queen, as he so often was, and it seemed he could endure no more, she wrote "Sir Spirit," commanding him not to be so "silly a soul" but to cheer up, "serve God, fear the king, and be a good fellow" and concluding her letter with the endearment — "God bless you, and long may you last."

Elizabeth's words to Cecil came from the heart but they were also the product of twenty-five years of experience. The personality so artificially confined to a single chapter was the work of a lifetime. The wily Elizabeth of 1583 was not the ingenue of 1558, and no one in that year had cause to know that the "unlooked-for miracle" was in the making; many subjects would not be entirely aware of it until the reign was over. All that could truthfully be said of Elizabeth Tudor at twenty-five was that she had "had good experience and trial of this world" and she had known "what it is to be a subject"; it now remained for her to discover what it was "to be a Sovereign."

FIVE

Our Noble Phoenix

Division kindled strife
Blest union quenched the flame:
Thence sprang our noble Phoenix dear,
The peerless prince of fame.
The Norwich City Gate, 1578

"VAIN" BUT "VERY ACUTE" was the shrewd judgment of one
observer of the new Queen upon the eve of her coronation.
Elizabeth needed to be both exceptionally acute and extraordinarily vain to imagine that a mere woman, whose intellectual accomplishments in a male society were neatly placed in
perspective by the aphorism "but can she spin?," could ever
infuse new life into the dying carcass of state. Within days of
her accession the Queen made the effort. In words as rich with
charm and promise as any she ever spoke, Elizabeth pronounced the guiding principle of her reign: "I shall desire you
all, my lords (chiefly you of the nobility, everyone in his degree
and power) to be assistant to me that I with my ruling and you
with your service may make a good account to Almighty God
and leave some comfort to our posterity in earth."

The appeal for counsel and advice on the part of a maiden of twenty-five who contrived to sound obliging and regal at the same time was the keystone of Elizabeth's design, but the first and most pressing item of royal business was to select the cast to support a leading lady who may have had no clear notion of the plot but knew exactly the part she wanted to play. The choice belonged exclusively to the new sovereign but the options were severely limited. In an island kingdom where possibly only 2,500 subjects enjoyed the economic and social status, let alone the intellectual or political qualifications, for the 1,200 or so royal offices financially "worth a gentleman's having," it was impossible to contemplate a clean sweep. Lordship, land, birth and custom controlled the mechanics of promotion as rigidly as they had done two centuries before. The Queen's authority existed only in league with a host of other interests, classes and corporations, with social and political privileges no less cherished than those of royalty. If the "well fashioned commonwealth" required every segment to "obey one head, one governor, one law, as all parts of the body obey the head, [and] agree among themselves," then the Queen must choose her councillors and lieutenants from among a self-perpetuating and exclusive body that placed family, title and estate above ideological purity or administrative competency. Elizabeth's flattering appeal "chiefly" to her nobility was little more than an acknowledgment of political reality; there were only about one hundred names from which to select the officers on whom her authority depended.

The Queen's household remained an unwieldy and unhygienic conglomerate, a thousand or more strong, with jealously guarded vested interests, services ineptly and carelessly rendered, shoddy and at times corrupt practices, and ceaseless petty squabblings. Except for the great officers of the court and those in close attendance upon the Queen, the management of the household was in the hands of a semiprofessional body who annually purchased, prepared and dispensed 1,240 oxen, 13,260 lambs, 310 pigs, 33,024 chickens, 4.2 million eggs, 60,000 pounds of butter and 600,000 gallons of beer. Elizabeth, however, had one advantage over her father, brother and sister — as a virgin queen her personal needs were relatively simple. What kind of reductions were introduced is difficult to say, since no historian has a clear picture of the true size or exact cost of the sixteenth-century household, but under Elizabeth there was no need for a second royal establishment to maintain a consort, a lord protector or a nursery. Moreover, Gloriana had no love for the costly, paramilitary prancing and preening which permeated her father's privy chamber, and she managed for most of her reign on £40,027 annually, a sum which Henry VIII, given the inflation, would have found totally inadequate.

Only in the Council was change apparent. Its size was slashed by a third but the conservative flavor remained much the same. In a body of twenty members, all but two had served close to the thrones of Elizabeth's predecessors; ten were holdovers from Mary's council, ten had served under Edward, and at least six harked back to Henry's reign. Four were landed magnates, relics of a feudal past when political loyalty was given to lordship and when kings were little more than oversized barons. Four others were political creations, promoted for their congeniality with kings and their services to the crown. Old William Paulet, Marquis of Winchester, had served, thrived and survived under three princes; he said himself that he was a man made not of oak but of willow that could bend with every religious and dynastic wind. William Herbert, Earl of Pembroke, despite his Protestant sympathies and highly profitable support of Northumberland, had continued to flourish under Catholic Mary and by 1558 was accounted one of the five wealthiest peers in the land — no mean accomplishment for a man who was said to have been unable to read or write. William Lord Howard belonged to England's second family, a clan that despite its treason rate and pronounced conservative and Catholic leanings was politically irrepressible. Lord William was Elizabeth's great-uncle, and the Howards never neglected family. She owed him much, possibly even her life. Except for the Earl of Bedford, a second-generation peer and Protestant emigré under Mary, the remaining eleven members were commoners — discreet, dedicated professionals who knew how to stage-manage, prompt and publicize Tudor monarchy. Sir Richard Sackville and Sir Francis Knollys were the Queen's Boleyn cousins; Thomas Parry had been her pushy but faithful servant and treasurer; all but one had started his career under her father; and all were a generation removed from their Queen in age, if not in sentiment. There were no religious radicals, no youthful and ornate royal favorites and no swaggering hawks. There were also no geniuses and, except for the indestructible Nicholas Wotton, no clerics. Cecil, Sadler, Petre, Mason and the rest were secular, practical politicians who followed Wotton's formula for success: "a happy medley of debonairness and complacency, reservedness and gravity."

Elizabeth was a keen judge of character who knew the value of loyalty, hard work and mastery of detail. She instinctively guarded her government from those flamboyant and opportunistic personalities who "neglected present profit in hope of greater matters, and so forsook the substance for the shadow." It is often asserted that Gloriana maintained a clear distinction between the gentlemen of her Council and the favorites of her chamber and never gave her young courtiers positions of administrative trust. Three of her gallants, however — Essex, Leicester and Christopher Hatton — later sat on the Council and the last two proved themselves to be highly adept at court politics. What the Queen disliked was too mercurial an intelligence, too caustic a wit and too innovative a spirit. Sir Walter Raleigh, Francis Bacon and Nicholas Throckmorton found the door to real power closed because in their several ways all three operated outside the ordained system of human and cosmological relationships which their sovereign lady had inherited and was determined to maintain to the end of her days. A less generous interpretation would be to say that Elizabeth preferred conventional mediocrity in her Council, if not in her closet, because it guaranteed the brilliance of her own wit and acumen. It was not altogether accidental that her first Lord Chancellor, Nicholas Bacon, displayed as his motto *Mediocria firma*.

The servant who most perfectly reflected in his private and ministerial life that debonair gravity urged upon Elizabeth's first Council was her Principal Secretary, Sir William Cecil. Few statesmen have left a vaster or more meticulous monument to their industry and skill; but despite the mountain of grumbling official correspondence, sighing private memoranda, copious minutes and lucid summaries of the pros and cons of state policy, Cecil remains a baffling and elusive figure, easily caricatured but difficult to analyze. The Polonian pomposity so often attributed to him because of his self-important tendency to instruct is deceptive. Sir William resembled an immensely dignified if somewhat grumpy gander, appearing to move majestically through the water but actually paddling away like mad beneath the surface, laying plans, spying on his rivals and scheming how best to manipulate his difficult mistress. Alas, only the formidable statesman has survived; the man with his frantic fears and urgent proposals can only be guessed at from the ripples on the water. Even so, Cecil's success is not difficult to explain. His mind functioned very much like that of his mistress, and almost alone among his colleagues he possessed the ability to formulate and present policy in a fashion ac-

ceptable to the Queen. Though he often parted company with
her anachronistic principles, Sir William was just as conservative and even more pessimistic in his estimate of political
morality. He was closest to his sovereign in the devious and
pragmatic ways in which he approached matters of state, and
he was her absolutely indispensable foil. While Gloriana glit-
tered in the spotlight of public applause, Cecil stayed in the
shadows, stage-managed the performance and pontificated
upon the exact degree of popularity becoming a subject: "I
advise thee not to affect nor neglect popularity too much; seek
not to be Essex and shun to be Raleigh." While Elizabeth ran
hot or cold, staged hysterics and indulged in royal temper tantrums, Cecil remained sorrowfully good tempered, seeking
never to "exasperate her Majesty, but [instead] to content her
mind and mitigate her displeasure." He accepted as gospel the
fact that he could achieve "more by his patience than ever he
did by his wit."

Everything about Cecil suited the Queen. Together they had
survived the guerrilla warfare of Edwardian politics and Marian Catholicism without indulging in treason or losing their
self-respect. He was Somerset's confidential secretary and a close
personal friend, but escaped his patron's fall by means both
questionable and obscure, and he reappeared under Northumberland as Sir William Cecil, Principal Secretary and a
member of the Council. Cecil's wares may have been "good and
saleable," as the Duchess of Suffolk unkindly pointed out, but
during the final days of the reign he openly opposed Northumberland's attempt to bar Mary and Elizabeth from the succession and signed Edward's device only at the express command
of the dying King. Hourly he anticipated imprisonment. He
went armed against assassins and contemplated fleeing into
Protestant exile, but in the end he survived the transition to
Catholic Mary, obeyed in the name of legitimacy and became,

in the words of one ill-wisher, "a creeper to the cross." Like
Elizabeth he placed obedience above the externals of faith but
not above conscience. He conformed under Mary in part because it was his duty but also because he was neither obsessed
by religious formulas nor committed to a monolithic truth. He
was, complained John Knox, very much addicted to "carnal
wisdom and worldly policy." Like his mistress he never revealed the exact nature of his belief and could be even more
obscure about it. When a critic accused him of being "a pagan
without sense or knowledge of God," he remarked: "What I
am indeed God only knoweth first, and secondarily myself, who
am, as you may be for yourself, partial." For Cecil, as for his
Queen, there was but one operating principle in religion: the
moment Henry VIII assumed the Headship of the Church of
England, the throne spoke for God no matter who wore the
crown. It was not for the common sort to take matters of creed
and ecclesiastical organization into their own unclean hands.
They must make do with conformity and prayer. If it pleased
Elizabeth to change the church, "it was well; if not, we were
to pray to God to move her heart thereunto, and so to leave
the matter to God and her Majesty."

Gloriana knew her "Spirit" well. In 1558 he had been the
surveyor of her estates for eight years at a salary of £20 per
annum, and in a sense he remained her loyal surveyor ever
after. Others at court might come and go, die or resign, but
Cecil went on for forty years — thirteen as plain Sir William
and Principal Secretary, twenty-seven more as Lord Burghley
and Lord Treasurer — giving to the Council and to the reign a
continuity and consistency which makes it almost impossible to
distinguish the responsibility for policy or disentangle the
Queen from her chief confidant and ministerial adviser. "I do
only keep on a course for show," Cecil once confessed, "but,
inwardly I meddle not, leaving things to run in a course as the

clock is left when the barrel is wound up." Such an approach
suited the Queen to perfection, but one wonders who wound
up the clock! For all his lamentations with "pain of sickness,
with grief of mind," for all his repeated offers to resign, his
mistress listened to him more than to any other man. He was,
it was said, "her code of laws." Again and again in her perplexity she turned to him, and during the Scottish crisis of
1564 she wrote privately, begging for help: "I am in such a
labyrinth that I do not know how to answer the Queen of
Scotland after so long delay. Therefore find something good
that I may put in Randolf's [the English Ambassador's] instructions and indicate your opinion to me." Invariably she
held to her own princely judgment but inevitably she turned
to Sir William for tactical advice — "let me know what you
wish me to do." Whatever their disagreements, Elizabeth
trusted Cecil, and though she scolded, threatened, blamed him
and made his life intolerable, she was always loyal. She openly
acknowledged that "no Prince in Europe had such a counsellor
as she had of him," and she graciously stooped to enter the door
of his sick room, making the compliment all the more memora-
ble by saying she would bow to no one else in all Christendom.
There is a delightful story that Elizabeth once laughingly
turned to Cecil and said, "With your head and my purse I
could do anything." Alas, the words are apocryphal but they
express better than any others the sense of partnership which
was built up over four decades of interdependence.

Sir William Cecil was a trifle parvenu but always a skilled
professional; the Earls of Shrewsbury, Arundel and Derby were
relatively domesticated feudal magnates; and at least a third
of the Queen's Council were Henrician Catholics. What was
conspicuously missing was a royal favorite, someone who enjoyed political influence and ministerial responsibility solely
because he was physically attractive. Traditionally there were

many paths to the prince's closet — shared interests, similar ages, latent or overt homosexuality — but when the monarch was a twenty-five-year-old maiden, a new dimension was added: *cherchez l'homme* who could touch her heart. In a sense, of course, all the Queen's servants, public and personal, were creatures of royal favor. In a personal monarchy, as Sir Francis Bacon explained, "the greatest subject that is or ever was greatest in the prince's favour" must stay close to the source of riches and offices lest absence breed "forgetfulness which gives way to wrath; and the wrath of a prince is as the roaring of a lion." The Earl of Essex and Sir William Cecil both knew that the court was the center of political life and that out of sight meant out of mind; worse, it meant out of pocket. Very early in the reign Cecil, when ordered to Edinburgh, wrote Sir Francis Throckmorton that "my friends abroad think I am herein betrayed to be sent from the Queen's Majesty." Forty years later Essex was complaining about much the same thing when he went campaigning in Ireland; he could, he said, protect himself from the enemy in front but "not on the back."

Royal bounty was "an essential virtue" of kingship. Cecil was as dependent upon the profits of the mastership of the wards and his license to export cloth and beer duty-free as was the Earl of Leicester upon the farm of sweet wines which paid for his personal secret service and secretariat, his town and country houses, his noble extravagance and his military obligations to the crown. For all his Renaissance arrogance and damnable feudal pride, Essex was constrained to cry out, "Between my ruin and my Sovereign's favour there is no mean," and Raleigh flippantly touched upon the core of political life when Elizabeth, in considerable exasperation, asked him "when will you cease to be a beggar" and he answered "when Your Majesty ceases to be a benefactor." Sir Walter knew what he was talking about: the Queen's favor had trans-

formed him from a threadbare soldier into a courtier worth
£3,500 a year and the landlord of 42,000 Irish acres, rented
from the crown for £66/8s/8p per annum.

Cecil and the other industrious ants of Elizabeth's Council
held office, income and estates at the Queen's pleasure, but they
did not command her heart. They were wedded to her service,
but the marriage was one of convenience. As yet no one possessed Elizabeth's love or could stake his political career upon
his comely limbs, shapely body and winning smile. In 1558,
however, one handsome devil stood in the wings: Lord Robert
Dudley, "light and greedy" but of "manly countenance." No
one could have been a less likely candidate. His upstart grandfather had died by the ax under Henry VIII; his father, the
Duke of Northumberland, and his brother, Lord Guildford
Dudley, had played with kingmaking and had paid the price;
and Robert himself had spent the first years of Mary's reign in
the Tower and had been ominously referred to as "the late
Lord Robert Dudley." Worse yet, he was married to a respec-
table landed heiress. Crippled though he was by family name
and matrimonial status, Lord Robert, like Elizabeth, had style.
He knew how to display his rather conventional talents and
marvelous masculinity to their best; and within hours of
Mary's death he appeared at Hatfield House mounted on a
snow-white charger, ready to serve his Queen both as a subject
and as a man. At first he was merely one among many aspi-
rants frantic to win favor where favor could earn such rich
rewards. But slowly quality or chemistry or "the hidden course
of the stars" began to take effect. It was one thing to appoint
him Master of the Horse and honor him with the Order of the
Garter, but quite another to tickle the back of his neck while
bestowing it. The envy of the court flared dangerously when
in October of 1562 he was awarded an annuity of £1,000 a year
from the London customs, but simple jealousy soon turned to

dread when Elizabeth began to "visit him in his chamber day and night." It took Lord Robert nearly three years to breach the council chamber and another three to reach the House of Lords as the Earl of Leicester, but within months of Elizabeth's succession professional bureaucrats and noblemen of ancient lineage discovered that they could not monopolize the Queen's ear, let alone her affections. Henceforth they would have to reckon with that most disturbing of political figures, the royal favorite, who could manage anything behind the scenes and was not bound by the arbitrary but predictable rules of court politics.

The result was that within weeks of the Queen's initial appointments to the major offices of state and the household, there began to emerge that most detested of monstrosities — political factions. It is sometimes argued that Elizabeth ruled by parties which she herself "made, upheld and weakened, as her own great judgment advised." The picture of a supremely wise and calculating Renaissance princess contriving by sheer intelligence to merge the chattering discord of personal and factional strife into a single harmonious chorus is part of the Elizabethan legend. A closer approximation of the truth would be that she was continuously struggling to disengage herself from factions, for political fragmentation and rivalry were inherent in a system built upon the assumption that the monarch was the sole wellspring of pensions, annuities, leases and gratuities. Cecil was absolutely sincere when he wrote Sir Thomas Smith in 1565 that he had "no affection to be of a party, but for the Queen's Majesty," and every servant of the crown would have said much the same with equal honesty. Unfortunately truth was clean contrary. Sir William could afford to be only of the Queen's party because he was already the head of a network of political influence which he guarded as zealously as any American political boss, but his continued control of the flow of crown patronage rested largely upon his ability to commit Elizabeth to his own faction. The court, as Cecil himself described it in 1566, was torn by "emulations, disdains, backbitings and such like." Clashes in the council chamber over state policy were matched by character assassinations in the privy chamber where rival parties sought to promote their own disciples, control the flow of royal bounty and whisper self-interested advice into Gloriana's ear. Cecil, as he proudly admitted, was "no baby," and after eleven years of close association, Elizabeth came to know her Principal Secretary well enough to comment that he often told her things about Robert Dudley "which turned out to be quite wrong."

The framework of Tudor society rested upon the twin pillars of paternalism and patronage, both of which supported an enormous growth of self-interest, deceit, dissension and factional bickering which no amount of pruning by the Queen could altogether control. Political success required the "mediation and remembrance of noble friends," especially those who possessed the keys to the sovereign's chamber. Bacon's advice to the Earl of Essex was to "win the Queen; if this be not the beginning, of any other course I see no end." Mr. Edward Dyer's counsel to Mr. Christopher Hatton in his constant battle to monopolize Gloriana's favor was even more Machiavellian. "Consider with whom you have to deal and what we be towards her who though she do descend very much in her sex as a woman, yet we may not forget her place and the nature of it as our Sovereign"; whomsoever the Queen dislikes, "the world followeth the sway of her inclination" without inquiring into the cause. No matter the personal cost, "never seem to condemn her frailties but rather to commend such things as should be in her, as though they were in her indeed." Then he presented the most seductive advice of all: "Use no words of disgrace or reproach" against your rival so "that, he, being the less provoked, may sleep, thinking all safe, while you do awake and attend your advantages."

The Queen had to be forever on her guard against such a hatchery of falsehood. She had little choice but to govern through political machines headed by those upon whom her rule depended, and she sanctioned a degree of factional murder and mayhem on the part of her nobly born lieutenants and favorites that is difficult to square with the storybook princess. The best she could do was to maintain a degree of independence of action, by playing one group against the other and by making her bounty as free as possible from factional pressure and political obligation. She used, wrote John Clapham, "many delays, but after long suit she gave voluntarily" on the sound political maxim that "in a prince it is comely to give unasked, but in a subject to ask unbidden." It was excellent politics but hard on her servants. When Cecil returned in August of 1560 from his diplomatic triumph in Scotland he was filled with gloom by what appeared to be his Queen's monumental ingratitude, for she refused even to pay his expenses and did nothing but criticize the terms of the treaty. "I omit," he inaccurately confided to Throckmorton, "to speak of my [dis]comfort of service . . . for her honour [I] oppressed myself with debt and have no consideration made to me." He did Elizabeth an injustice; five months later she gave him as a "free gift" the mastership of the wards.

Gloriana was exceedingly well informed. Occasionally her advisers withheld information but it is difficult to be sure how successful they were, for the Queen delighted in the motto "I see but I keep silence." At times there were moderately effective conspiracies to conceal the sexual indiscretions of her favorites, and late in the reign Robert Cecil admitted that he had tried to cover his tracks so that his mistress might not suspect he "looked to anything but [her] service." A certain amount of judicious misrepresentation eased the wheels of politics, but it was dangerous to presume too much. Elizabeth might for a time turn a blind eye on the peccadillos of her gallants or might even overlook corruption in high office, but she had a long memory and a sharp ear as Sir Henry Unton discovered in 1593. He was a member of the Essex faction in Commons, and Essex sought to persuade the Queen to grant Sir Henry a government position. Elizabeth would have none of it and charged Unton with "popularity," indicating that she knew every particular of his parliamentary speeches "as the anatomy, the pots and pans, and such like."

Patronage made the Elizabethan world go round, and each patron headed a political empire stretching from the innermost reaches of the chamber to the outermost shires of the kingdom. Of all the key figures at court Sir William Cecil and Lord Robert Dudley represented the two extremes: professional versus amateur, bureaucrat versus courtier, pessimist versus optimist, statistician versus gambler, diplomat versus soldier. They were in effect different sides of the Queen herself, the one appealing to her cautious, crablike, yet perversely perceptive mind; the other to her wayward and incomplete instincts as a woman. Both appeared during the first days of the reign; Cecil as Principal Secretary on November 17, Dudley as Master of the Horse on the eighteenth. In a symbolic sense Lord Robert, for all his flamboyance and style, was always a day behind Mr. Secretary, but both grew old with their mistress and stayed with her until the end of their days — one thirty years, the other forty — and they even learned to work in tandem, harnessed by a royal lady who understood them and was unswervingly loyal to both.

Important as Sir William and Lord Robert were to be, neither held the center of the stage on the day Catholic Mary died; the man to whom Elizabeth owed the most was Nicholas

Heath, her sister's Lord Chancellor and Archbishop of York. As the highest official of state and the second ranking ecclesiastic of the realm, Heath was confronted with an agonizing choice, his duty to God or to Henry's dynasty, for no one could believe that Anne Boleyn's daughter had any love for Rome even if she had attended mass at her sister's command. Heath was the last of his species, a dying breed in a secular world: an ecclesiastical statesman. He represented in his person and career everything that was most admirable and most despicable about the old church: its secularism, belly wisdom and involvement in affairs of state on one side, and its moderation, cosmopolitanism and humanism on the other. Heath was an Henrician prelate through and through, and fortunately for Elizabeth he was absolutely loyal to the Tudor throne. Three hours after Mary's death he summoned both Lords and Commons to proclaim Henry's daughter Queen: "God this present morning hath called to His mercy our late Sovereign Lady, Queen Mary: which hap, as it is most heavy and grievous unto us, so have we no less cause another way to rejoice with praise to Almighty God, for that he hath left us a true, lawful and right inheritrice to the crown . . . which is the Lady Elizabeth . . . of whose most lawful right and title . . . we need not to doubt."

It was difficult to strike the exact balance between mirth and mourning, lest subjects "should seem either to sorrow for her which was to succeed or to joy for her which was dead." There were many who felt nothing but joy that Mary with her "heading, hanging, quartering, and burning" was mercifully gone to her Catholic reward, but graver minds felt "sorrow for her which was to succeed," for behind the rejoicing were a host of ugly pigeons coming home to roost, not the least being those fervent soldiers of the Lord who had spent the last five years cooped up in Calvin's Geneva. If burning and axing had been

the mark of Catholic bigotry under Mary, the odds seemed
high that Protestant zealots under Elizabeth would seek their
revenge, and popish atrocity be repaid in full with Puritan
inhumanity. An inexperienced girl of twenty-five would soon
have to face stern men from both religious extremes who were
quite willing to see "the entire destruction of England" if it
were necessary "for the great glory of God and the welfare of
Christendom." Equally serious was the shame of Calais, lost to
France in a war from which Englishmen had returned "as men
dismayed and forlorn." Elizabeth's untried government had
the unpleasant choice of continuing a fruitless and unpopular
conflict or signing a degrading peace and blackening the memory of Agincourt and Crécy. Either way there seemed to be
little hope of winning the respect of subjects or rebuilding the
self-esteem of the realm. For a decade England had been drift-
ing, paralyzed at home, humiliated abroad. Prices were spiral-
ing, the coinage was debased, the crown lands plundered and
the government loaded with debt. If Elizabeth were to survive
and avoid bankruptcy she would have to reduce expenditures,
retrench her commitments and live within her means. But
what then of the bounty so essential to a king; of her reputation as a "gentlemen's queen" and a "liberal dame" who would
satisfy every aspiration; and above all, what of that excellent,
if costly, advice to "gratify your nobility and the principal
persons of your realm . . . whereby you shall have all men of
value in your realm to depend only upon yourself"? Indeed
Sir William's chronic pessimism — "What her Majesty will determine to do only God I think knoweth" — was singularly
appropriate in 1558, and all agreed that "our remedy must be
prayer, for other help I see none."

Elizabeth did not call upon the deity for aid. Instead she
did the next best thing and required the astronomer royal, Dr.
John Dee, to cast her horoscope, observe the stars and calculate

the most propitious date for her coronation. He determined upon Sunday, 15 January, 1559, which was, judging by hindsight, an extremely felicitous reckoning. The ceremony lasted three frantic days: the official entry into the Tower; the formal progress through the city, replete with speeches, prayers, floats, tableaux, pageants and rapturous crowds; and the climax in the Abbey where the Queen received the crown of St. Edward upon her head, the sword of state around her waist, the orb and sceptre in her hands and the blessings of God upon her reign. A regiment of seamstresses, carters, saddlers and carpenters had worked for over a month. In the Abbey seven hundred yards of blue carpeting fell prey to eager souvenir hunters even as the Queen walked by. The scarlet costumes of the household cost £5,794 and it took another £3,958 to bedeck the great officials of state. In all Elizabeth spent £16,741/19s/8¾p, a sum that not only reveals the Queen's love of exact accounting but also her willingness to invest money where it did the most good — in magnificent staging. Throughout the pageant Bess was superb. The coronation had been turned into "a stage wherein was showed the wonderful spectacle of a noble hearted princess toward her most loving people," and she responded to the full, "condemning no person, neglecting no office and distributing her smiles, looks and graces so artfully that there upon the people again redoubled the testimony of their joys."

Elizabeth radiated an aura of self-confidence — the Spanish Ambassador called it vanity — for she was certain history was on her side and that time and good fortune would see her through. Others, however, were not so confident. Those who argued that it was against natural and divine law for a woman to "reign and have empire above men" had only to refer to the sad spectacle of the previous half-dozen years when mercy had been confused with justice, indecision had paralyzed policy, and piety had deteriorated into savage dogmatism. Moreover,

the future would be littered with evidence of feminine dis-
asters: Mary of Guise was to die amid Scottish civil war; Catherine de' Medici would leave behind her a kingdom sunk in
misery and torn by ideological atrocities; and Mary of Scotland
would perish on the block. Only the Virgin Queen of England
would stand as an exception, but in 1558 there was no reason
to expect such a miracle. John Knox for one was convinced
that only an "extraordinary dispensation of God's great mercy"
would ever permit the successful dominion of a woman. The
Lord, however, works in marvelous ways, and Elizabeth's dynastic competition was handicapped from the start. Though
the English crown was "not likely to fall to the ground for
want of heads that claim to wear it," the contenders were all
members of the monstrous regiment which Knox so abhorred.
Of the three Protestant Suffolk claimants, Catherine Grey was
silly and arrogant, Mary Grey was dwarfed and stupid, and
Margaret Clifford was retiring and unambitious. The Catholic
Lennox-Douglas clan was scarcely better. Margaret Countess of
Lennox was Henry VIII's niece by the marriage of Margaret
Tudor and Archibald Douglas, Earl of Angus, and the Countess was aggressively ambitious for her handsome son, Henry
Lord Darnley. Unfortunately by Catholic law Margaret Douglas was a bastard, since the Pope had annulled her parents'
marriage. Finally, there was Mary Queen of Scots, Henry's
grandniece by his sister's first marriage to James IV of Scotland, but Mary's mother was French, the Stuarts had been
omitted from the Tudor succession, and worst of all she was
married to the Dauphin of France. Not even the staunchest
English Catholic could stomach the thought of a daughter of
France upon the Tudor throne. Fortunately for Elizabeth her
brother-in-law held the same view. He preferred an English
princess of uncertain religious sentiments to a Scottish queen
of unimpeachable orthodoxy controlled by France, and for the

first ten years a capricious deity arranged that Hapsburg Philip of Spain should remain the vigorous champion of Anne Boleyn's daughter.

From the start fortune, with benevolent perversity, proceeded to line the blackest international clouds with the most unexpected silver. The continental war into which England had been drawn by Mary, and from which only disgrace and bankruptcy could be expected, against all logic proved a partial blessing. The Hapsburg-Valois struggle guaranteed that Philip would counter French pressure upon the Pope to have Elizabeth declared a heretic and bastard incapable of succeeding to the throne. Even when peace was signed in April of 1559 at Cateau-Cambrésis and Philip contracted to marry Elizabeth Valois of France, Gloriana's luck held. During a joust in honor of his daughter's wedding, Henry II's eye was pierced by a splinter of wood and within days he was dead. In the blinding of an eye the entire international balance of power was upset. France took a giant stride towards thirty years of religious and civil war, and Philip was driven back into the hands of England, for the Dauphin was a boy of fifteen and his wife's ducal relatives, the predatory and militantly anti-Spanish House of Guise, ruled in Paris. Philip was soon to learn that his English sister-in-law was the "daughter of the devil," but he endured her cheerful lies, doubtful casuistry, beguiling assurances and deliberate misrepresentations, partly because his interests were absorbed in the Mediterranean by the Turkish menace but also because he was faced with a moral quandary: which was worse, an enemy to his faith or to his European hegemony? Spain's perplexity was England's greatest defense.

The Queen was fortunate in two other matters. She reaped the benefits as well as the disadvantages of twelve years of mistakes and misrule. The men on whom she chose to depend were not merely moderates filled with the spirit of compromise, they were an historic unit, every one of whom — whether a Henrician Catholic or Protestant — was a product of the break with Rome. It was the shared memory of twenty-five years of social and political instability as well as the sight of smoldering corpses on Smithfield Green that established a bond between the young sovereign and the leaders of society which had not existed since 1547 or even perhaps 1533, the year of Gloriana's birth. What lent strength to the Queen's position and would give distinctive coloring to her reign was the fact that Elizabeth was the youngest of her generation and would live to be the last.

Cautious men were in control, but they were immeasurably aided by the moderation of the two extremes: in 1558, and possibly never again, Catholics could be depended upon to be graceful losers and Protestants restrained victors. Time and circumstance were crucial. The resurgent tide of Catholic militancy and martyrdom had not yet touched English shores. Rome was too much entangled in European politics and too worried by the infidel at its doorstep to concern itself with the spiritual plight of Englishmen. A handful of brave men maintained that the doctrine of legitimacy was a slender reed upon which to stake the collective soul of an entire church, and the Marian Bishop of Winchester dared to preach at Mary's funeral service that "the dead deserved more praise than the living," but he spoke in Latin and the warning went unheeded. The Catholic church in England was as hollow as its Latin, and with Mary's death the structure collapsed. Of the two men who might have saved it, Nicholas Heath chose duty to the memory of the old King and Reginald Cardinal Pole was called to his Maker four hours after the Queen died. Pole's death was only part of fortune's blessings, for it seemed as if the church's will to live was as weak as the Cardinal's. When Pole died five bishoprics were already vacant; by the end of the year four more prelates had died, leaving an episcopal bench paralyzed in leadership, almost halved in numbers and incapable of resistance.

Elizabeth and Cecil had every reason to believe that the old church was destitute of the spirit of martyrdom and would willingly return to Henry's nonpapal Catholicism, and in that confident expectation they approached the most pressing problem of the new reign and began the restructuring of the English ecclesia. They were wrong on two counts. The church lacked the will to fight for the old faith but it would not sanction a return to schism. Nicholas Heath and the rest had learned a bitter lesson, and they refused to make the same mistake twice: "Whatever is contrary to the Catholic faith is heresy; whatever is contrary to unity is schism. . . . It is the same thing, so far as schism is concerned, to do a little or to do all." Try as she might, Elizabeth could not persuade the Archbishop to remain on her Council or to help in turning the religious clock back to the days of Henry VIII. Instead, he and his fellow clerics resigned their sees en masse. The refusal of the Marian prelates to cooperate was a body blow to the Queen's religious solution which, like almost everything she did, had been modeled on her father's experience. Equally serious was her miscalculation of the returning Puritan exiles and their fervent supporters in the House of Commons. Her Protestant divines, though devoted to their Queen, were just as difficult as the Marian bishops: they also would not go back in time. And so Elizabeth compromised.

No daughter of Anne Boleyn could give in to her sister's prelates; whatever the cost the Royal Supremacy had to be restored. Consequently Elizabeth had no option but to cut her religious settlement to suit the Puritan style, and step by step she retreated into what an unsatisfied radical minority scornfully described as a "leaden mediocrity," a Protestant creed decently dressed in the time-honored vestments of Catholicism. To pacify the Catholics she softened the title of supremacy from Supreme Head to Supreme Governor of the Church of England, but to win the militant Protestants she had to accept the Edwardian Prayer Book of 1552. The left-wing triumph, however, was not an unqualified victory. To the unmistakably Protestant administration of the sacraments — "Take and eat this in remembrance that Christ died for thee and be thankful" — was added from the 1549 Prayer Book the much more conventional words: "The body of our Lord Jesus Christ which was given for thee, preserve thy body and soul unto everlasting life." By the addition of a single sentence, the Elizabethan service became both a sacrifice and a remembrance, acceptable to anyone who believed with the Queen that there was "only one Jesus Christ, and all the rest is a dispute about trifles." Elizabeth settled for "a mingle mangle" in matters of dogma, but to the horror of her Protestant divines she held the line on church ritual. The ancient regalia of the priesthood, which the Puritans considered the "livery of Anti-christ," was carefully preserved from further Protestant purification.

Puritans liked to think that their youthful mistress "openly" favored their Calvinistic cause but had held back because of the political inexpediency "of allowing any innovations." If Elizabeth gave her "Protestant gentlemen" such a sanguine notion, she was only proving Simeon Renard's earlier assertion that she was not always to be believed in matters of religion. In later years Gloriana made it clear that she infinitely preferred "Catholics who did not place their conscience in antagonism to the state" to Puritans bent on enforcing their own interpretation of God's word. The Queen herself was never afflicted with her father's tender conscience, which so often descended into pedantic and ferocious enforcement of God's law, nor was she plagued by the doubt and guilt that drove so many of her contemporaries to excesses of faith. She lacked that direct emotional association with God which inflates the soul with a sense of egocentric fulfillment and union with God's purpose upon earth. Hers was a tolerant and unfanatical approach, deeply personal but never soul-searing. She believed that each Christian must ultimately make his own treaty with God and the exact terms were up to the individual. Mental reservations had kept her safe under Mary, and now in her own religious solution she aimed at a broad, often confused, theological structure, intended to satisfy as many mental reservations as possible. Elizabeth understood that most people are willing to live with theological contradictions and to work out their own terms with eternity, either at the moment of death or on a regularized basis throughout their lives.

Her settlement is invariably called a success, especially the speed and ease with which it was formulated and adopted: the Act of Supremacy, the Revised Prayer Book and the Act of Uniformity were all prepared, debated and enacted by April, and Parliament was adjourned on May 8, 1559. Yet compromises are not always successes. The religious settlement of 1549 had been a disaster which satisfied nobody, and Elizabeth's solution might have fared no better save for two important if contradictory points. First, the Queen was adamant that her settlement was final. She as well as her Puritan ministers had reached a point beyond which they were unwilling to go. Second, her solution, far from destroying Protestant expectations, permitted hope to live and thrive: "Now is the time for the walls of Jerusalem to be built again in that kingdom, that the blood of so many martyrs, so largely shed, may not be in vain." By the sheerest good fortune the exact balance had been struck between obscurity of doctrine that permitted tender Protestant consciences to accept the religious formula, knowing as they did that they had won the substance if not the form of the battle, and imprecise half-measures which allowed the hope of future clarification and improvement. For the time being the Protestants were content to pray that "the divine spirit" would enlighten their Queen; Catholics were satisfied that she would demand no windows into their souls; and Elizabeth herself was pleased with what she had achieved — the "over rule" of her church. Even if she had failed to emulate her father's theological settlement, her religious authority was just as complete as his: "Our excellent Queen . . . holds the helm and directs it hitherto according to her pleasure." She had begun, she later said, "as it became me, with such religion as both I was born in, bred in, and, I trust, shall die in."

Elizabeth's own contribution to the religious settlement is far from clear. She may have stood alone and been slowly maneuvered into a compromise by her Council in league with the radicals in and out of Parliament, for she obviously did an about-face during the debate and capitulated to Puritan opinion. Moreover, in later years she remarked that she only accepted the 1552 Prayer Book because of Protestant concessions made over the issue of ecclesiastical vestments and ornaments. On the other hand, it is equally certain that she was not totally isolated. At crucial moments she had the support or at least the advice of William Cecil, who boasted that the final solution was largely his. "I must confess," he wrote Throckmorton, "that I am thereof guilty but not thereby at fault and thereto I will stand as long as I shall live." Whoever was ultimately responsible — Queen or minister — both were determined that the settlement should be final and irrevocable. The Supreme Governor of the church had spoken and henceforth she expected both Protestant and Catholic to obey. In retrospect Elizabeth looks strong and magnanimous in her handling of the religious crisis, partly because time has effaced the indecision, hesitation, undignified haggling and temper tantrums,

and partly because the settlement was achieved without recourse to what Gloriana feared might be irreversible decisions.
Except for the renewed break with Rome, it was possible for
the Queen to convince herself that her options were still open
and, if necessary, the Supreme Governor, but no one else, could
renegotiate the terms of the compromise. She felt herself to be
in control of the situation.

Foreign policy was another matter. Tudor charm, charisma
and divinity might gull the souls of dutiful subjects, but they
were of little avail in a world of international cannibals in
which England, a mere "half island," was "but a morsel among
those choppers." War and her handmaiden diplomacy involved
irrevocable steps and risky gambles which no amount of hedg-
ing of bets or loading of dice could entirely cover, and Elizabeth was invariably at her worst when it came to issues over
which she had no control or which required clear choices between alternative policies. She delighted in the preliminaries
of diplomacy, sparring with ambassadors, throwing dust in her
opponents' eyes and endlessly spinning out negotiations so as
to escape the final, unalterable moment of commitment. Unfortunately sovereigns, as Elizabeth discovered within months
of her accession, eventually had to commit themselves in a
world where the conditions of survival were constantly changing.

In November and December of 1558 the "first and principal
point" to think about was peace, and the measure of England's
desperation was Elizabeth's reluctant agreement with the
unanimous opinion of her Council that Calais would have to
be sacrificed for the sake of her treasury. France, not Spain,
seemed to be the European colossus "bestriding the realm, one
foot in Calais, the other in Scotland" where James V's widow,
Mary of Guise, and her French soldiers ruled in the name of
the sixteen-year-old Queen of Scots. Peace became official in

April of 1559, but within three months the international scene
had so changed that Elizabeth's reign, far from inaugurating
an era of peace, opened with a call to war. During the next
four years, the Queen had to scrape together a war chest of
more than £750,000 when her bankrupt exchequer had an
annual revenue of only £200,000 and a parliamentary subsidy
that averaged no more than £50,000 a year.

In the spring of 1559 Scottish lairds, their clannish souls
made even more militant by John Knox and his Calvinistic
creed, rose in force against Mary of Guise and her pro-French
and Catholic policies. Civil war had been endemic in Scotland
for nearly two decades, and for two years the "congregation of
the lords," as the Protestant and parliamentary militants called
themselves, had been in open revolt. What precipitated the
crisis for Elizabeth was their appeal for English arms and
money. Cecil immediately perceived a unique, if dangerous,
chance to remove the French dagger at England's back, link
the two halves of the island in "perpetual amity," and strike a
blow for Protestantism. It was, he said, imperative to "kindle
the fire, for if it be quenched the opportunity will not come
again in our lifetime." Unfortunately the Principal Secretary's
dreams clashed head-on with his sovereign's most cherished
prejudices, for the Queen was suspicious of Calvinists by instinct, abhorred traitors to their princes on principle, and detested John Knox in particular.

The indefatigable Mr. Knox was as insistent in his demands
for English support as he was uncompromising in his main-
tenance of God's exact word, and he wrote Cecil that "in the
bowels of Christ Jesus I require you Sir, to make plain answer"
when, where and how much aid the Scottish rebels could expect from Elizabeth. It is questionable whether Cecil would
have ever been able to persuade Gloriana to send help if chance
had not played into his hands. On July 10 Henry II died,

thereby throwing France into the chaos of minority government and catapulting Mary of Scotland and her Guise relatives into what could be interpreted as a direct threat to Elizabeth's own security. Cecil took immediate advantage of the
situation, and in August presented his policies to the Queen in
terms she was most likely to understand: it was necessary to
defend herself from an international conspiracy directed at her
crown. To avoid her objection that it was "against God's law
to aid any subjects against their natural princes," he wisely
dropped all mention of a Protestant crusade and concentrated
on his mistress's historic rights as feudal overlord to interfere
in Scottish affairs, and upon the threat that France would turn
Scotland into a staging ground for the conquest of England. It
was a masterful document, for it appealed to the Queen's fears
for her own safety and to her desire to follow in her father's
footsteps: Henry himself had claimed feudal suzerainty over
Scotland. Cecil was immeasurably helped, moreover, by Mary
Stuart's blatant and insulting assumption of the title and arms
of the Tudor crown, a defiant disregard of legitimacy which
went far to ease Elizabeth's scruples about aiding and abetting
her cousin's rebellious subjects.

Gingerly Elizabeth took the first tentative steps into the
chilly waters of Scottish diplomacy. Three thousand pounds
were distributed in absolute secrecy to the rebel leaders, not as
a gift from a generous Queen but as a personal loan from the
English Ambassador. It was scarcely the plain answer that John
Knox had demanded, but it was the best the Secretary could
manage from a monarch who found the entire Scottish adventure profoundly distasteful to her inherited principles and
disastrous to her pocketbook. Cecil was in a frenzy, arguing
that "the best counsel is to make haste" lest the Scottish rebels
revert to their ancient and predatory ways and sell out to the
highest bidder and the French be given time to reinforce their

troops at Leith, the fortified port of Edinburgh. Elizabeth refused to be maneuvered into action except by degrees, each costly step taken in order to safeguard a previous one and each new involvement inevitably committing her to some further expense. First it was simply a matter of money. Then in December Admiral Winters, on the pretext that he had been driven north by the weather, was sent to blockade Leith in order to prevent French reinforcements. Elizabeth ducked all responsibility, however, and ordered her luckless Admiral to attack the French only on his own initiative and not on hers. Finally, in March the Duke of Norfolk was given permission to cross the border with an invading army. Gloriana's prevarications and petty economies seemed interminable to her Secretary, who tearfully insisted that his mistress not lose the chance of a lifetime. "With a sorrowful heart and watery eyes" he besought her Majesty "to pardon this my lowly suit" to proceed "in this matter for removing the French out of Scotland." It was, he lamented, quite impossible for his conscience to "give any contrary advice," and he begged permission to be allowed to serve his sovereign in her "kitchen or garden."

Nothing seemed to go right, and the deeper Elizabeth moved into the morass of Scottish civil war the more it appeared that the deity was punishing her for lending support to rebels and traitors. The Lords of the Congregation were consistently defeated in battle; the cost of military intervention soared, and in May English troops were ignominiously repulsed in their major assault on Leith. Cecil was sunk in gloom and poured out his woes to Throckmorton — "The Queen's Majesty never liketh this matter of Scotland. You know what hangeth thereupon; weak-hearted men and flatterers will follow that way. . . . I have had such a torment herein with the Queen's Majesty as an ague hath not in five fits so much abated." Worse was yet to come. On May 26 he was ordered north, to extract his Queen from an expensive and accursed enterprise into which his own dangerous policies had unwittingly pushed her. It was exactly at this point that fortune intervened. Mary of Guise died on June 17, and almost in the same dispatch Cecil learned of Philip of Spain's disastrous naval defeat by the Turks in the Mediterranean. The Catholic cause in Scotland was now leaderless, the French could no longer hope for Spanish support for their Scottish policy and their blockaded troops in Leith were starving. Suddenly, from moaning that his journey seemed "very strange and diversely judged," Cecil managed to get almost everything the English demanded. In the Treaty of Edinburgh the French abandoned the use of the arms and title of England, thereby recognizing Elizabeth's right to her father's throne; there was a mutual withdrawal of all but a handful of troops from Scotland; and all French military bases were demolished. The Scottish government was securely placed in the hands of a pro-English and Protestant faction, and the working agreement between Elizabeth and the Lords of the Congregation was preserved. Everyone, in fact, viewed the treaty as a diplomatic triumph except the Queen, who was unimpressed by the victory of Calvinism under the odious Mr. Knox, was acutely embarrassed by the thought of becoming the champion of militant international Protestantism, and was bitterly disappointed that Cecil had not succeeded in getting the French to return or pay for Calais.

Calais may have been engraved upon Mary Tudor's dying heart, but for the first years of the new reign it was rarely off Elizabeth's mind. In her Scottish policy, she had been at constant odds with a majority of her Council, had acted with the greatest reluctance only when she felt her personal and dynastic interests were at stake, and had shown not the slightest interest in pursuing a consistent, let alone aggressive, foreign policy. But the Queen was her father's daughter, and given the

proper stimulus she could be swept off her feet by the chimera
of European conquest — if it could be done with maximum
glory and minimum expense. Years later she maintained that
she had never sought to "advance my territories and enlarge
my dominions, for [though] opportunity hath served me to do
it . . . my mind was never to invade my neighbours. . . ."
She had forgotten, however, the time when she had been en-
ticed onto the rocks of continental invasion by the siren voice
of Calais.

The occasion was again death within the ranks of royalty.
Francis II died in December of 1560 of an abscessed ear and was
replaced by his neurotic nine-year-old brother, Charles IX, who
was completely under the influence of Catherine de' Medici
the Queen Mother. Suddenly the political monopoly of the
Guises was broken and replaced by a precarious balance between the three semi-independent feudal houses of Guise,
Montmorency and Bourbon. In France, unlike England, family
vanity, provincial loyalties and religious paranoia merged into
an unholy trinity of warring baronial armies, religious fanaticism and monarchical paralysis, which in May of 1562 plunged
the kingdom into civil and ideological conflict. As early as
1559 the English resident Ambassador, Nicholas Throckmorton, had been piously and enthusiastically preaching intervention on the optimistic grounds that "now is the time to spend
money." It seemed that France had become a second Scotland
where the mighty Guise could be cut down to size and the
papal dragon cast out. God-fearing Frenchmen, it was said,
would welcome the soldiers of the Lord even if they came from
across the Channel. Presumably what was good for the Scottish
goose was also good for the French gander, and the Huguenot
party offered to sell French soil in return for English silver and
armed men.

Suddenly Elizabeth and Cecil found their roles reversed. She thought the temptation irresistible and the Principal Secretary reverted to his usual grumpy pessimism, darkly referring to any war in France as "the bottomless pit" and pointing out that the Queen could not even afford to fortify Plymouth Harbor. Elizabeth was all for immediate action, and when she encountered opposition in the Council it was reported that she grandly announced "that if they were so much afraid that the consequences of failure would fall upon them she herself would take all the risk and would sign her name to it." On the face of it Elizabeth's words were most uncharacteristic, and the Spanish Ambassador may have exaggerated the Queen's militancy, but her enthusiasm was closely tied to Robert Dudley's growing influence. Lord Robert was wildly eager to prove his metal, regain England's tarnished military honor and unite the historic policy of continental aggrandizement with England's newer role as champion of militant Protestantism abroad. Moreover Elizabeth felt that succouring French rebels was not the same as conspiring with her blood cousin's treasonous subjects; there was no talk of unseating Valois Charles, only of regaining what was legitimately her own — Calais. Here was her great chance to equal her father, and in April of 1562 Throckmorton optimistically wrote, "The Protestants must be handled and dandled" so that they might be moved to give "the Queen possession of Calais, Dieppe or Newhaven, or perhaps all three."

By July the terms had been established: 140,000 crowns and 6,000 men to help defend Dieppe and Rouen in return for Newhaven, which was to be held until Calais could be handed over to the English. Elizabeth's troops arrived in October under the command of Dudley's older brother, the Earl of Warwick; and much to everyone's satisfaction England was once again back on the continent. Within weeks it was clear that a disastrous miscalculation had been made. Rouen and Dieppe

fell to Catherine de' Medici's troops in November; the Huguenots were roundly defeated in pitched battle and their leader
captured; and in March the warring sides patched up a peace
and joined together to evict the hated English from Newhaven. By July of 1563 an English garrison decimated by disease faced a French army 40,000 strong, bent on enforcing the
Queen Mother's pronouncement that if Elizabeth did not return the city voluntarily "God will enable us to take it by
force." Once again Gloriana backed down. She swallowed her
pride and surrendered the port in return for the honorable
departure of her troops, who sailed home with nothing left of
England's proud excursion into continental warfare except the
plague, which promptly spread throughout the kingdom.

Elizabeth had severely burned her fingers, but she was neither vindictive nor, in this case, did she try to shift the blame
onto her Council. Perversely Robert Dudley remained in high
favor and in October actually won his way into the Council
chamber, but Elizabeth had learned her lesson. The disaster of
Newhaven had not been sufficient to unseat Lord Robert but
it did cement the alliance between the Queen and her Principal Secretary: henceforth both were unswerving isolationists.
In his Scottish policy Cecil was a tight-little-islander, while
Elizabeth was determined to preserve her diplomatic freedom
of action by saving her pennies and resisting any further at-
tempts to persuade her to indulge in European conquests or
religious crusades. Every instinct that had made her hesitant to
sanction change, listen to masculine warlike advice or risk
precipitous action had been confirmed by the surrender of
Newhaven. She was now more adamant than ever in her determination to let sleeping dogs strictly alone, to bury her head
in the time-honored sands of legitimacy and divinity, and never
again to cooperate with those monsters of nature, traitors to
divinely constituted authority.

It had not been a very brilliant start. After three years all that can be said is that the dramatis personae had appeared and that the Queen, her ministers, and the various rival factions about the throne had all gotten to know one another. The pattern of government had slowly begun to emerge. Her servants suffered cruelly from their sovereign's unpredictable frivolity as she learned how to turn delay, half-truth and inconstancy into the fine art of government, but they doggedly, albeit respectfully, continued to cajole and harry her along a predetermined course. Elizabeth soothed their ruffled pride, beguiled with artful words their religious scruples, rewarded their loyalty with political responsibility and wealth, and attempted with varying degrees of success to maintain her independence and impose her majestic will upon those who served her best. It was a baffling and makeshift arrangement based on a host of unanswered questions and postponed issues which, like the Mad Hatter's tea party, had its own twisted logic. But it had one glaring flaw — it took no account of the possibility of the Queen's marriage or death. In October of 1562 the honeymoon abruptly ended in "great terror and dreadful warning" when Elizabeth was struck down by smallpox and the kingdom had to face a domestic crisis in which Gloriana and her subjects sat squarely and inflexibly on different sides of the tea table.

The Word of a Prince

> Henry the fourth [of France] . . . in a jovial humour
> told a Scottish marquis there were three things inscru-
> table to intelligence: 1. Whether Maurice then prince
> of Orange (who never fought battle, as he said) was
> valiant in his person. 2. What religion himself was of.
> 3. Whether Queen Elizabeth was a maid or no.
> — FRANCIS OSBORNE, *Historical Memoirs*

WHEN ELIZABETH'S FIRST Parliament gathered on January 25,
1559, expectations ran high and Lord Keeper Nicholas Bacon
in a speech laden with rhetorical embellishments voiced the
enthusiasm which filled every loyal breast: how happy Englishmen were that God had presented them with "a princess to
whom nothing — what, nothing? No, no worldly thing — was
so dear as the hearty love and good will of her subjects." The
Lord Keeper was right in theory but wrong in fact. There were
two matters which Gloriana privately regarded as dearer than
the love and good will of her subjects: matrimony and the succession to the throne. At almost the same instant that Bacon
was mouthing his fulsome oratory, Count de Feria, the Spanish
Ambassador, was making an equally fallacious prediction:

"Everything depends on the husband this woman takes." His logic was unimpeachable but his assumption unwarranted. Neither the Ambassador nor the Lord Keeper contemplated the highly improbable event of no marriage at all. Elizabeth Tudor's persistent refusal to wed is as perplexing as her father's mulish determination to marry Anne Boleyn, and the ingredients of the enigma are strangely similar — reasons of biology, psychology and state. The only statement that can be made with any certainty is that the Queen stood alone, in opposition to the overwhelming opinion of the wisest minds of her Council, the historic prejudices of her subjects, and what everyone else regarded as the best interests of her kingdom. Mr. Thomas Sargrove expounded no more than the self-evident when in the Parliament of 1559 he maintained that "nothing can be more contrary to the public respects than that such a Princess, in whose marriage is comprehended the safety and peace of the Commonwealth, should live unmarried, and as it were a Vestal Virgin."

As the sixteenth-century saying went, "There belongeth more to marriage than two pair of bare legs," but in Elizabeth's case the bare legs may have presented an added element to an already complex problem. If that Bourbon Lothario Henry IV of France many years later regarded his sister sovereign's maidenhead as one of the three great mysteries of his day, historians need not feel obsessively inadequate when they fail to unravel the puzzlement of the Queen's physical and emotional response to sex. Setting aside doubtful physical malformities, probable menstrual difficulties, a possible father fixation or other psychological disturbances, it is reasonably fair to say that Guzman de Silva, the most observant of a series of Spanish ambassadors, put the problem in its most succinct and accurate form: "The Queen would like everyone to be in love with her but I doubt whether she will ever be in love with any-

one enough to marry him." De Silva's analysis was based on
Elizabeth's flaming romance with Lord Robert Dudley, but
there is plenty of evidence supporting his proposition.

From the first days of the reign, the Queen had been as forth-
right and honest about matrimony as it was politically possible
to be, and in her answer to the parliamentary plea that she
"take some man to your husband, who may be a comfort and
help unto you, and a consort in prosperity and adversity," she
indulged her talent for the dramatic and said: "To satisfy you,
I have already joined myself in marriage to a husband, namely,
the Kingdom of England." Whereupon she drew her coronation ring from her finger, loudly exclaimed "behold the pledge
of this my wedlock and marriage with my Kingdom," and announced that she was content to live and die a virgin. It was
magnificent staging but nobody believed her, and in considerable exasperation she informed de Silva that it was ridiculous
to believe "a woman cannot live unless she is married, or at
all events that if she refrains from marriage she does so for
some bad reason." The Queen's views were dangerously anti-
social and ran counter to the rooted conviction of her century
that as a woman she needed a husband to instruct her in her
wifely duties, and as a ruler she required a man to lend the
throne the necessary "print of government" and to secure the
dynasty with an heir. There could be no refuting this last
point, and worried Mr. Secretary Cecil prayed urgently to God
to "send our mistress a husband and by time a son, that we
may hope our posterity shall have a masculine succession."

Had it been possible for a sixteenth-century husband to be
simply a royal stud, Elizabeth might indeed have married for
the sake of posterity, but like everybody else she appreciated
the fact that when wives were queens, husbands must needs be
kings, which made the selection of a spouse well-nigh impossible. Nobody could settle upon an acceptable candidate. A for-

eigner was attractive to many, partly for diplomatic reasons
and partly because he would be a stranger to English party
politics and might be politically gelded by treaty or training.
There were, however, two insurmountable obstacles to foreign
marriage. A prince worth the risk of upsetting the domestic
balance would unfortunately have to be a Catholic. Except for
the Swedes and the Danes there were no other kind, and no
one could contrive a way to satisfy a Catholic consort married
to a heretical queen in a Protestant country. Even had moderate men of pragmatic faith been able to locate a Valois or
Hapsburg scion of flexible conscience and worked out some
amicable arrangement for mass to be said unofficially at Whitehall, there was the Queen's insistence that any future husband
be inspected in the flesh. Like her father she maintained that
marriage touched her too closely to "trust portrait painters";
and here was the dilemma, for no self-respecting princely candidate was willing to come to England for an interview for fear
of being rejected.

The domestic selection was even more precarious. Cecil in
one of his tidy pro-and-con memos neatly summed up the over-
riding disadvantages of a marriage within the kingdom when
he wrote with Dudley expressly in mind that "nothing is increased by marriage of him, either in riches, estimation, power.
. . . He shall study nothing but to enhance his own particular
friends to wealth, to offices, to lands and to offend others." De
Quadra, the Spanish Ambassador, put it more brutally when
he said that "the Duke [of Norfolk] and the rest of them cannot put up with his being king." Much as councillor and courtier, clergyman and squire loyally and romantically yearned
that their sovereign lady dispose herself to marry for the sake
of a godly imp to secure the succession, they could not avoid
the unhappy realization that man and wife "must have one
heart, one will, and one mind" and "keep no secrets from each

other." Such a picture of connubial bliss and interdependence was altogether too dangerous to be allowed. In this the Queen fully agreed; she had no intention of sharing her crown with the man who shared her bed.

Whatever psychological and physiological inhibitions to marriage there may have been, matrimony itself contained the greatest barrier. Elizabeth had already negotiated one alliance with God on the basis of blood and heritage in which she had been given dominion over men. It was unthinkable that she should now enter into another holy contract in which the terms, by definition, were reversed. Eliza fancied herself a Vestal Virgin, a nun in God's service, but if the truth were told, she really had in mind the role of a prioress — humble to God and dedicated to the service of His church but all-powerful over those under her. Sir James Melville, the Scottish Ambassador, in an oft-quoted remark laid bare the heart of the issue when he boldly informed her: "I know the truth of that, madam, you need not tell me. Your Majesty thinks that if you were married you would be but Queen of England, and now you are both king and queen. I know your spirit cannot endure a commander." Elizabeth never answered Sir James, but she came close to admitting the truth of his diagnosis when seventeen years later she gave as her reason for not marrying the Duke of Alençon the argument that "I shall not be able to govern the country with the freedom and security that I have hitherto enjoyed."

The full complexity of the marriage problem both for Elizabeth and her subjects came to a head in the person of that comely if ineligible suitor Lord Robert Dudley. For months Parliament had been tactfully urging matrimony, to which the Queen ritualistically responded with vague promises and postponements. Initially her brother-in-law Philip had been the most promising candidate, and Count de Feria assured her that his Holiness would readily grant his faithful son a papal dispensation to marry his deceased wife's sister. Elizabeth met Philip's diplomatic advances with the pointed reminder that history had already been upset as a consequence of violating Leviticus, and she had no more faith than her father had had in the Pope's authority to dispense with scriptural prohibitions. Elizabeth was "the best marriage in her parish," and when Philip shifted his marital attentions to Elizabeth Valois, he sought to keep a family foot in the door by urging the attractions of his Hapsburg cousin, Charles Archduke of Austria. Hapsburg nuptials waxed hot and cold but were, for the time at least, laid to rest in 1560 when the Queen wrote the young man's father that she had "no intention of abandoning a single life." In England the gossip was exactly the opposite, and everyone was desperate for fear that Gloriana had finally settled on a most unlikely lover.

In the eyes of the English nobility no one could have been less suitable as a royal consort than Lord Robert. Descended from a "tribe of traitors" and blatantly opportunistic, he was guaranteed to outrage the sensibilities of the old nobility and arouse the blackest suspicions of civil servants and rival courtiers alike. He was detested for his arrogance, violence and good looks, but while his wife lived he was not regarded as dangerous and was cast solely as the first of Elizabeth's paramours: an oversexed creature of the court who was rumored to pay as much as £300 for the pleasures of one of the gentlewomen of the Queen's chamber. In the spring of 1559, however, there were sinister stories afoot, reports that his wife had a "malady in one of her breasts and the Queen is only waiting for her to die to marry Lord Robert." In November the Spanish Ambassador picked up talk that Dudley had "sent to poison his wife." Less than a year later Cecil was "so full of melancholy" that he spoke of resignation if God did not "send her

Majesty understanding," and he informed the sympathetic de Quadra that Dudley was "endeavouring to deprive him of his place" by governing all at court, and that Lord Robert's wife was "taking care not to be poisoned." When the Ambassador reported these words he could not have heard the sensational news: on September 8, 1560, Amy Dudley was found dead of a broken neck at the bottom of the stairs in a house seemingly devoid of servants. The coroner brought in a verdict of accident, local gossip opted for suicide, the court and international circles spoke openly of murder, and Lord Robert became the leading candidate for the Queen's bed.

Suddenly a reign which had begun with controlled and cautious moderation collapsed into sordid backstairs scandal, and Mary of Scotland, respectably married and properly shocked by the frivolity of Elizabeth's court, set the style of international gossip by dismissing her English cousin as the Queen who was "going to marry her horse-keeper, who has killed his wife to make room for her." Sir Francis Throckmorton in Paris was in a frenzy, as foreign courts delighted at Elizabeth's discomfort and commented that nothing less could be expected in a heretical land. He wrote to Cecil in his anguish, begging him to stop the marriage at any cost, for should such a mésalliance take place "God and religion will be out of estimation; the Queen discredited, condemned and neglected; and the country ruined and made prey."

Throughout the fall and winter of 1560 tongues were busily wagging. Tales of the Queen's secret pregnancy were being circulated; Throckmorton bombarded his friends at home with warnings of dire calamities "if Her Majesty do so foully forget herself in her marriage"; and it was reported that both Dudley and his mistress looked haggard and "perplexed" by the flood of malicious gossip. Elizabeth did not in the end "foully forget herself," and both the Queen and her councillors learned a lesson. Henceforth almost all serious advice on the subject of Gloriana's marriage would be given with the unwritten rider that she select a husband from outside the realm. Elizabeth had to face the fact that she was not as other women. Even if she possessed perfectly normal sexual drives, she was still politically abnormal; marriage to Dudley's masculinity could not be squared with her own divinity and inheritance, and by 1564 Cecil was contentedly reporting that the insurmountable impediment to her marriage was the fact that Lord Robert was "by birth the Queen's subject." Thirteen years later, when she was diplomatically wooing the Duke of Alençon, Elizabeth said almost the same thing: "Dost thou think me so unlike myself and unmindful of my royal majesty that I would prefer my servant whom I myself have raised, before the greatest prince of Christendom, in the honour of a husband?" By 1576 the question was easily answered, but in 1561 most people thought it a very near thing indeed.

The prospect of marriage to Dudley may have exposed the impossibility of an English bridegroom, and it certainly left the Queen more convinced than ever "to end her life in virginity," but it also raised doubts about the succession. Not even Gloriana could reign forever. This fact was made dramatically clear on October 10, 1562, when she came down with smallpox. "Death," as she said, "possessed almost every part of me." The world had been reminded of the mortality of princes when within seventeen months two kings of France had died — Henry II in July of 1559 and his son Francis II in December of 1560. Two royal deaths in France had led to feudal and religious wars from which every predatory neighbor, including Elizabeth, had sought to profit. The same thing could happen in England, especially now that the widowed Mary Queen of Scots was free to confront her cousin as a double threat — heir presumptive to her throne and the second best match in Europe.

The script for history's most dramatic confrontation was not yet complete, but the moment Francis II died, his eighteen-year-old, auburn-haired, vivacious widow became the femme fatale of Europe, tragic, alluring and politically pure poison. Nowhere was her presence regarded as more fatal than in Puritan circles in London, where good Protestants looked upon her succession to the Tudor throne as a catastrophe to their spiritual and worldly well-being. Married to Francis she had been unthinkable as Queen of England; now as the unmarried Queen of a bleak and impoverished realm she was the leading claimant, attractive both to those who dreamed of a united Britain and to those who believed in strict legitimacy irrespective of religion. Though Mary had grander aspirations, in the end she had no option but to leave the center of Renaissance culture and return to her damp and chilly homeland, determined to win with her Stuart charm a kingdom caught in the vise of John Knox's stern morality, and to claim her right as Elizabeth's legitimate successor.

From the moment Mary set foot on Scottish soil the "mad world," gloomily predicted by Protestants in both kingdoms, commenced, and the Scottish Queen began to exercise an unholy influence upon English political life which was to last for the next twenty-seven years and earn her the appellation of Dragon of Discord. Her captivating presence across the border immediately began to polarize Tudor politics, placing renewed pressure on Elizabeth to marry so as to thwart her Catholic cousin's ambitions, and turning Protestant eyes towards the Suffolk sisters in the event of the Queen's death. Marriage and the succession had always been as intricately intertwined as any lover's knot. Now they were further snarled by factional politics and personal ambitions. Cecil favored the Protestant Suffolk claim but for diplomatic reasons was willing to see his Queen married to a Hapsburg Catholic prince; Dudley quietly

sought to sabotage any marriage except to himself, and supported the Stuart claim largely because he knew his mistress's
unreasoning antipathy towards her Grey cousins and hoped
thereby to undermine Cecil's political influence at court. As
for Elizabeth, she retired into a maidenly silence about her
marriage and an unpredictable oscillation on the subject of
the succession, at one moment imprisoning the Lennox family
and the next quashing Catherine Grey's sub rosa marriage to
the Earl of Hertford and declaring their son to be a bastard.
Then came the scare of October 1562, which once again
brought the matter of the succession out into the open and
back into Parliament.

The government was desperate for money, and three months
after the Queen's illness Parliament was called upon to help
finance the costly Newhaven venture. Elizabeth got her subsidy
but she also received three separate petitions from Parliament,
each begging her to "marry where it shall please you, to whom
it shall please you, and as soon as it shall please you," and
asking her permission to discuss and legislate upon the succession so as to avoid "factious, seditious and intestine war."
To the first petition she answered in words both gracious and
majestic. She spoke of her womanly wit and bashfulness but
warned them of her "princely seat and kingly throne" insti-
tuted of God. There was, she said, no "need to prate" about
her death; and she would "take convenient care of you all" in
this matter which touched her so much more than anybody
else. She would be "neither careless nor unmindful" of their
safety, but she was "determined in this so great and weighty
a matter" to defer her "answer till some other time. . . ."
Upon further advice she would give further answer. To the
next petition she was far more outspoken, angrily informing
them "that the marks they saw on her face were not wrinkles
but pits of smallpox and that although she might be old, God

could send her children as He did to Saint Elizabeth," and she warned that "if she declared a successor, it would cost much blood to England." To their third request she simply sent word that she had not forgotten their suit and recommended "young heads to take example of the ancients" and be patient.

Elizabeth was in a devilish position. For the first but not the last time she stood alone, operating on principles peculiar to herself and utterly at odds with the collective wisdom of her Council and Parliament. In religion and foreign policy she had made concessions, but her marriage and the succession were personal concerns, not affairs of state or matters of expediency, and they involved the nature of her sovereignty. Her father had settled the succession as if the crown had been a piece of furniture and had violated the historic rights of legitimate descent by ignoring the Stuart claim. What Henry could do, Elizabeth on the same grounds could undo. Legitimacy had brought her to the throne and legitimacy must needs succeed her. From the perspective of the blood succession Mary Stuart was her only possible heir, but to have said so would have brought her into direct confrontation with a highly vocal and well-organized Puritan majority in Parliament determined to protect itself from a Scottish Jezebel. In refusing to heed her ministers' advice or give comfort to the tender consciences of her over-wrought subjects, the Queen as usual made appeal to the prag-matism born of her own political experience. She disliked any mention of death, especially her own, and viewed all discus-sion of the succession as tantamount to preparing her shroud and winding sheet. She had not forgotten the calculating well-wishers who had crept to Hatfield House in anticipation of her sister's death. In 1564 de Silva was convinced that Elizabeth would never name her successor because of these memories, and four years earlier Cecil had told de Quadra that his mistress had no intention of nominating Catherine Grey because of the saying that "the English run after the heir to the crown more than the present wearer of it." There was no alternative but to stall and beguile, and in April she worked hard to get the tone of her final speech exactly right before proroguing Parliament. She would, she assured Lords and Commons, keep her prince's word "unspotted" and give answer to their petitions. For her marriage, a "silent thought" sufficed: Though virginity may be "best for a private woman, yet do I strive with myself to think it not meet for a Prince. And if I can bend my liking to your need, I will not resist such a mind." On the subject of the succession she was even more bewilderingly obscure, and assured her listeners that she expected to die in peace "which cannot be without I see some glimpse of your following surety after my graved bones." It was not one of Elizabeth's best performances, but she was young and still learning, and Parliament had to be satisfied for the time with "some glimpse," whatever that might be.

Gloriana in her divine, if devious, wisdom had evolved her own unique solution to the succession, which seemed eminently sensible to the Queen but to no one else, either then or now. It involved no less than the marriage of Mary Stuart to Lord Robert Dudley, the one bachelor in all England who might be predicted not to covet the Scottish beauty. On the face of it, a spy in Mary Stuart's bed, satisfying her desires, blunting her Catholicism, keeping her off the matrimonial marketplace and supplying a half-English heir to the thrones of both England and Scotland made a good deal of dynastic sense to a Queen determined not to name her successor but to see to it that her throne went where God had ordained it — to the Stuart line. Both Dudley and Mary were embarrassed, for both had far greater marital ambitions. Lord Robert had by no means given up hope of his English Eliza, and Mary was outraged at the notion of wedding her rival's hand-me-down. Out of Elizabeth's Freudian scheme Dudley earned himself the Earldom of Leicester — it was conferred in October of 1564 to polish up his pedigree and make him more attractive as a Scottish stud — and Mary to her everlasting regret met, fell in love with, and married the "handsome, beardless and lady-faced" Henry Lord Darnley. It was in all likelihood Dudley, casting about for ways to escape the sacrificial marriage altar, who persuaded Elizabeth to grant Darnley license to visit Scotland. Instead of neatly resolving the riddle of the succession, Elizabeth now found herself in the midst of a crisis which made her encounter with Parliament in 1563 seem an amateurish dress rehearsal. "Woe worth the time," wrote the English Ambassador, "that ever the Lord Darnley set foot in this country." Mary Stuart was married on 29 July, 1565; thirteen months later Elizabeth gloomily reported that "the Queen of Scots is lighter of a fair son while I am but a barren stock." Worse, Gloriana was thirty-three years old. With this figure firmly fixed in their minds, plus the knowledge that the two Catholic houses of Stuart and Lennox were linked in the person of young Prince James, Lords and Commons reconvened in Parliament on October 3, 1566.

Elizabeth had promised she would "bend" her mind to matrimony, and she had kept her word in the confident knowledge that it would never be put to the test. Even as Parliament met, the courtship of the Archduke Charles ran hot and heady but got nowhere, for every Cecilian diplomatic argument in favor of a foreign match could be countered by a Dudleyan question about the dangers of permitting a Catholic husband to hear mass in the Queen's chapel. In 1566 subjects were beginning to despair of their sovereign's marriage, but their very desperation bred a renewed determination to secure the succession in the Protestant line and to force Gloriana to name her successor. Protestant sentiment throughout the realm and the Puritan majority in Commons would not tolerate Mary Stuart on the throne; the very "stones in the street would rebel against it." On the issue of her marriage Elizabeth could always pose as the innocent victim of factional politics and unavoidable diplomatic delays. On the subject of the succession, however, she could not hide behind party strife; her only counters to parliamentary demands were vague assurances that she would yet marry and haughty statements that she would not be "buried alive" by naming her heir. So cautious, halting and uncertain in some things, Elizabeth was obdurate when she felt her principles to be at stake.

The situation was serious enough when a queen's "ruling" and her subjects' "service" were in open conflict, but the struggle took on a new and more dangerous dimension when matters of conscience and parliamentary rights united to threaten the crown's prerogative. The very essence of Elizabethan government was placed in jeopardy when Commons sought first to initiate discussion on the succession, a subject expressly forbidden by the sovereign, then attempted to blackmail the Queen into submission, and finally spoke presumptuously of the liberties of free speech. Money stood at the root of the parliamentary offensive, for Elizabeth was nearly bankrupt. Sir Ralph Sadler presented the government's argument that the House had an obligation to fortify the kingdom financially against "the malice of the enemies and adversaries of God's gospel" which "waxeth very hot," but it was not the business of Commons to treat of the succession which concerned the Queen alone. Prayer, not legislation, was the approved recourse for those who would influence a monarch: "Let us pray to God in whose hands the hearts of princes are." The Lord generally helps those who help themselves. Supplication to the deity and to the Queen had gotten Commons nowhere in 1563, and now the Lower House answered: "No! No! We have express charge to grant nothing before the Queen gives a firm answer to our demands." Such words were lèse majesté, and Elizabeth could not make up her mind whether she was more furious with her Protestant devils in Commons who were confirming all her worst suspicions about Calvinism, or with the Duke of Norfolk who had tactlessly raised the subject of the succession in the full Council.

The battle shifted to the Upper House when the peers sent a delegation headed by Norfolk to implore the Queen to declare her mind or send Parliament home. Noble prayers had no more effect than plebeian threats, and Elizabeth coldly told them, "My Lords, do whatever you wish. As for me, I shall do no otherwise than pleases me. Your bills can have no force without my assent and authority." Gloriana knew her constitutional rights and the noble lords retreated to discuss the subject of their defiant sovereign with a committee from the Lower House. Together they returned for a second audience. If peers and commoners thought that there was safety in a collective front they were sadly mistaken, for Elizabeth put on a first-class display of royal temper. She called Norfolk a traitor, the Earl of Pembroke a "swaggering soldier," and when she scolded Dudley and he fell to his knees, fervently assuring her that "he would die at her feet," she answered with impeccable logic that "that had nothing to do with the matter." She then stalked out and threatened to put the entire lot under house arrest.

Gloriana had not finished. Ten days later she spoke her mind to thirty members of each house who had been ordered to attend her in her chamber. The speech is justly famous and one on which the Queen took great care, selecting her words with precision, restraining her original anger but displaying her flair for rhetoric in a masterpiece of majestic scolding. Who, she asked, are these "unbridled persons," and "scabbed sheep" to speak of the succession? Had she failed her kingdom

that subjects should now castigate her? "How have I governed
since my reign? I will be tried by envy itself. I need not to
use many words, for my deeds do try me!" As for her marriage,
she would never break her word; she would marry "if God
take not him away with whom I mind to marry, or myself, or
else some other great" event happen. Having given her royal
word but, in fact, having given nothing, she then lectured them
like so many schoolboys on the history of the succession, the
dangers of naming a successor and the divine nature of her
office. For their benefit she pointed out a simple political truth:
"If you should have liberty to treat of it, there be so many
competitors" to the throne that "some would speak for their
master, and some for their mistress, and every man for his
friend," and the ensuing debate would make the passage of a
money bill seem trifling in contrast. There could be no compromise with divine authority, and the Queen ended her
address as she had begun; she would never be forced to do
what she did not have a mind to do. She took her stand on the
basis of God and her father's right; only when it was convenient would she "deal therein for your safety, and offer it
unto you as your Prince and head, without request; for it is
monstrous that the feet should direct the head."

Next day Sir William Cecil conveyed Gloriana's words to
the House, but no amount of skillful editing could transform
the "roaring of a lion" into the song of a nightingale. The
Queen's command to drop the subject was met first with sullen
silence and then with a menacing question — "whether her
Highness's commandment, forbidding the Lower House to
speak or treat any more of the succession . . . be a breach of
the liberty of the free speech of the House, or not?" The query
was never allowed an answer. Elizabeth grudgingly backed
down in principle if not in fact; she graciously discovered that
"her commandments were not necessary," for she was sure that

her "good and loving subjects" would "stay themselves upon her said answer, without pressing her Majesty any further therein at this time." By implication, if not by principle, she had surrendered a fraction of her prerogative — the exclusive right of the monarch to settle the succession without parliamentary discussion — but she had recouped the loss by appealing to her subjects' personal loyalty and their willingness to refrain from exercising their right for her sake. Historically it was a dangerous concession, but it was immediately effective in avoiding a constitutional confrontation which nobody wanted or completely understood. Whose wisdom prevailed we do not know, but Elizabeth always sensed the need for saving face, and she was never a pedant as to form so long as the spirit suited her. The actual words of the solution have a Cecilian ring to them, but it was the Queen who got what she desired — the end of further discussion of the succession.

For all her royal courage and stately stomach, Elizabeth always had her priorities strictly in mind: all the armies, subsidies and historic rights in the world were worthless pieces of armor compared to the steel of her subjects' love, and when Parliament rose on January 2, 1567, she sought in carefully chosen words to regain the constitutional ground she had lost without spoiling the ecstasy of her people's affection. She started off with a patent but winsome lie: only her hatred of "counterfeiting" and "dissimulation" induced her to speak once more of the succession and the liberties of subjects. As for the first, there were some who lewdly endeavored "to make all my realm suppose that their care was much, when mine was none at all." She excused such impudent untruth on the grounds that the cause was weighty and the perpetrators witless. As to liberties, who was so simple as to doubt "whether a Prince that is head of all the body may not command the feet not to stray when they should slip?" Lords and Commons had been "sore seduced" to believe that her prohibition was illegal. She did not blame them for their ignorance; she merely pitied them, asking only "to see my subjects' love to me more staunch" than the burdens of her office were "great." Then she ended with a warning: "Let this my discipline stand you in stead of sorer strokes, never to tempt too far a Prince's patience." Within seventeen months everyone's patience was tempted to the breaking point, for on 18 May, 1568, Mary Queen of Scots crossed the border into England and the question of the succession was once again squarely deposited on Elizabeth's doorstep.

Gloriana's political principles were rooted as much in emotion as in reason, and her refusal to name her successor may have had more to do with an atavistic reluctance to sign anything which admitted her own mortality (we have no last will and testament for Elizabeth) as with any practical concern for the danger of establishing a rival political center, which by definition must always look to the future. Up to 1568 political calculation and irrational instinct were in harmony, which made it easier for the Queen to resist Puritan and parliamentary pressure. Thereafter the Queen's position became even less tenable; Mary of Scotland's insatiable desire for the Tudor throne and her presence in England made it politically mandatory to discourage Stuart dreams by proclaiming a legal heir. The succession had from the start presumed the eventuality of the Queen's death, but now a more immediate and more sinister note was struck: the growing dread that the dynasty might be overthrown and the Protestant faith destroyed by the assassin's knife. At home subjects took to prayer to give their Queen perfect health, "for with her good estate we all breathe and live and without her we all strife and perish." On the continent the Duke of Alva ominously advised Philip of Spain to risk sending troops to install Mary Stuart on the throne only "if the Queen of England should die, either a natural or any other death."

Elizabeth may have had her own convoluted solution to the problem of the succession — to postpone any answer in the hope it would ultimately resolve itself — but she was a very astute female and was fully aware of the inherent dangers of her policy. Sometime during 1565 she wrote Sir Henry Sydney making an oblique but perceptive reference to her Stuart cousin's presence in Scotland. "I pray God your old strange sheep late (as you say) returned into fold, wear not her woolly garment upon her wolfy back. You know a kingdom knows no kindred — *si violandum est ius regardi causa*. A strength to harm is perilous in the hand of an ambitious head. Where might is mixed with wit, there is too good an accord."

The story of Mary Stuart's marital and monarchical undoing is quickly told. It may defeat the imagination to detect exactly what it was that Elizabeth did right to produce such extraordinarily disproportionate successes, but it takes no miracle of analysis to discern where Mary went terribly wrong — she mixed love and murder in proportions fatal to her throne. Henry Darnley was soft and handsome but he was also greedy and vicious. Though styled King Henry, he was a paper monarch, sovereign by right of his marriage, and in Scotland as in England no man could abide the epigram:

> Megge lets her husband boast of rule and riches
> But she rules all the roost and wears the breeches.

Darnley's drunken sense of political and husbandly impotence was directed at his wife's overly private French secretary, David Riccio, who dined alone with his mistress, shared her confidences and some said her couch as well, and in March of 1566 a particularly brutal murder took place. Kicking and screaming,

"Seigneur Davie" was dragged from behind his mistress's skirts and cut down. Mary neither forgot nor forgave, and eleven months later she had her revenge. On February 9, 1567, Darnley, incapacitated by what was probably a syphilitic attack, was strangled outside his house moments after it was blown to pieces. Six years before, Mary delighted at the possibility of Lord Robert Dudley having done away with his wife in order to marry his Queen. Now the evidence began to mount that a Scottish princess had done away with her husband to marry her lover. Two and a half months after the murder, Mary was dramatically abducted and "raped" by her husband's assassin, Protestant James Hepburn, Earl of Bothwell, whose sexual achievements and political ambitions made Dudley's escapades seem amateurish. Mary's role has never been adequately explained, but the accusation that she was both a murderess and an adulteress was difficult to deny when a mock trial was staged in which Bothwell was acquitted of homicide, and a month later, on May 12, Mary married her abductor. Protestants and Catholics alike were deeply shocked, and soon the streets of Edinburgh rang with the demand to "burn the whore." In June she was imprisoned and forced to abdicate in favor of her young son; the following May she contrived a most improbable escape; was disastrously defeated in battle; and on the sixteenth, shorn of her titles and her golden red hair, she fled across the border to England with nothing but borrowed clothes on her back and Tudor blood in her veins.

Until Mary Stuart's disheveled and unexpected arrival in England, Cecil and the rest of the Council had been cautiously jubilant over the events across the border, but the same cannot be said for Elizabeth. She was appalled that Mary had made royalty appear ridiculous and lectured her cousin on the need to appear unbiased and just. Nevertheless she could not sanction Scottish sedition against "their sovereign lady," even after

Mary had cast off the last shreds of self-respect by marrying Bothwell. Cecil answered her "as wearily as he could," but Gloriana grew so indignant that she openly threatened war and was only restrained from armed intervention by her fear of driving the new Scottish Regent into the arms of France and by the timely accident of a painful "crick in her neck," which aggravated her temper but kept her from interfering with Cecil's delicate handling of the situation.

Righteous and princely anger over the fate of a cousin safely imprisoned in Scotland was one thing; her bodily presence in England was another, and Elizabeth's initial reaction to Mary's supplication to hear her just cause and assist her in recovering her rightful authority was anything but auspicious. She sent her "two torn shifts, two pieces of black velvet, two pairs of shoes and nothing else." She did, however, give her princely word "that neither your subjects nor any advice which I may receive from my own councillors" would persuade her to endanger Mary's life or honor. Again Bess was willing to go it alone and defend her royal word in the face of national interests and her own security. What to do with her unwanted guest on the other hand was a riddle to which neither the Queen nor her advisers could find an adequate answer. "Her Majesty can neither aid her, permit her to come to her presence, or restore her, or suffer her to depart before trial." The suggestion of a trial or hearing to judge the charge that Mary was a murderess and her subjects justified in deposing her in all likelihood came from Cecil, but it suited the Queen perfectly, for it permitted her to play the part of an impartial feudal overlord. It also gratified her sense of dynastic superiority to hear her rival's frank and humble confession and her promise to mend her ways. Best of all, it delayed any final decision. The Scottish Queen yielded to the proposal of a hearing because, though she did not as yet know of the existence of the Casket Letters "proving" her complicity in Darnley's death, Mary possessed a trump card which she knew her sister sovereign would respect — the infallible word of a princess.

The "trial" ended in a draw. The Scottish rebels were told that nothing had been brought against them to impair "their honour and allegiance" but that nothing "had been sufficiently produced" against their sovereign "whereby the Queen of England should take evil opinion of the Queen, her good sister." As usual Elizabeth had sought to have her cake and eat it too: to do nothing that would actually restore Mary to her Scottish throne but at the same time not to go back on her word of honor. The judicial hearing had postponed but not resolved the enigma, and the Spanish Ambassador voiced the prevailing masculine opinion that "it is certain that two women will not agree very long together."

De Silva was quite right; Mary and Elizabeth were on a collision course. Conditions in England seemed peculiarly susceptible to what Mary had to offer — promises, smiles and dreams of a throne — and she was soon busy spinning a web of intrigue. There were "many simple men" who might yet "be carried away with vain hope and brought abed with fair words." The same economic, social and ideological tensions which were destroying France had begun to operate in England. The tempo of religious hysteria was accelerating, giving substance to Puritan fears that "no papist can be a good subject," and forcing Catholics to choose between loyalty and conscience. In the northern shires the spectre of feudal rebellion was taking shape as the old nobility, awkward in their unbecoming role of court aristocrats, sought to reestablish the good old days of baronial independence. Sir William Cecil had cause to draw up an inventory of lamentations, in the wake of the parliamentary stalemate of 1566, in which "dangers of sedition in summer by persons discontented" was the last and most prophetic item on the list. At court factional hatreds erupted into near violence and it was predicted that "there are communications going on amongst the aristocracy here, which threaten a storm. . . ." Under the circumstances Mary could write with quiet confidence to the new and militantly Catholic Spanish Ambassador, Guerau de Spes: "Tell your master that if he will help me, I shall be Queen of England in three months and mass shall be said over the kingdom." All Mary needed was a suitable fly, and in September England's ranking peer, Thomas Howard, fourth Duke of Norfolk, took the "sweet bait" and walked into the web.

In ten years of rule Elizabeth had made only one serious mistake: she had failed to win the heart of the richest and most titled gentleman of the kingdom. It almost seems as if she had gone out of her way to antagonize her ducal cousin. Thomas Howard had been passed over when her Council was first formed, and he did not join that select body until 1562 when, rather insultingly, he was brought in to balance Dudley's promotion to the inner circle of advisers. During the Scottish campaign he had been in nominal but highly restricted command, and he was ignored when Dudley's brother was placed in charge of the Newhaven expedition. In great bitterness and with some justification, the Duke burst out that "her highness hardly thinks anything well bestowed on me be it never so small." Possibly the Queen thought that Norfolk had quite enough already. He jogged along on £6,000 a year, and when he took as his third wife the Catholic widow of Thomas Lord Darce, he joined the estates of two of the largest landowners in the realm. It was a tactless but scarcely idle jest when Howard assured his sovereign that while at home on his own estates he was as rich and powerful as any king of Scotland. Gloriana may have blundered in ignoring the kingdom's only surviving duke, but she did not misjudge him. Thomas Howard was an

aristocratic anachronism whose wealth, title and birth constituted a political alternative to Tudor autocracy. Personally
loyal to the Queen by principle, Norfolk nevertheless possessed the instincts of his kind, the inbred conviction that the
divinity of kings was merely an extension of the divinity of
peers. He had just enough ambition to feel politically neglected
but not enough intelligence to perceive that he was persistently
being used by those less naïve and less obtuse than himself. He
was in effect the most dangerous of all sixteenth-century political beasts, an injured and therefore unpredictable noble mag-
nate.

Given the short life expectancy of Tudor dukes, Norfolk
should have known better than to dabble in treason, but in
seeking to marry the Queen of Scots he imagined he saw his
political chance. He could not resist the role of champion for
a charming but deadly lady in distress. It flattered his pride,
and it resolved the problem of the succession. Norfolk would
be bedded to a queen; Catholic Mary, married to a Protestant
Englishman, would be no threat to the English church; and
moderates of both faiths could rally to her support, thereby
avoiding the possibility of civil war in the terrible event of
Elizabeth's death. This happy solution, however, had three
important defects. It took no account of Cecil and his powerful
left-wing Puritan allies, who were politically and religiously
committed to the Suffolk line; it overlooked Mary's designs
upon her cousin's throne; and, most important of all, it left
the task of informing Gloriana to Norfolk and he funked the
job. Elizabeth was a formidable lady, indeed something more
than a man and less than a woman, and Howard hesitated to
tell her of the proposed match. Norfolk must have expected a
tirade, for the Queen was an inveterate dynast, and he must
have known that she would correctly view any marriage to
royalty as potential treason.

Norfolk was such a simple-minded traitor that he has had his passionate defenders but, as Sir Francis Walsingham coldly observed, it was extraordinarily difficult to believe that England's richest and rankiest peer wanted to marry a deposed monarch and murderess-cum-adulteress whom he had never seen simply out of inordinate love for her Stuart smiles. Exactly when Elizabeth learned of her cousin's marital schemes is impossible to say, and it raises questions as to how much was successfully concealed from her and how much she chose to ignore, either in the expectation that matters would never come to a head or in the hope that she could arrange things so that Norfolk could back down without losing face. The Duke had already assured her that he would rather go to the Tower than marry "such a person where he could not be sure of his pillow," but by June of 1569 he had long since forgotten his words. The proposed marriage was an open secret and the Council dangerously divided. Dudley and Cecil secretly took opposite sides, but in public they both endeavored to play the honest broker. Throughout the summer Elizabeth gave Norfolk every chance to broach the subject, first pointedly asking him whether he could tell her any "news of a marriage" and later giving him a "nip" and saying "to take good heed of his pillow." Finally in September, Dudley with tears and sighs divulged all, in a way carefully designed to keep his own shirt-tails clean and to place the blame firmly on Norfolk. The Duke as a consequence was roundly berated by his sovereign, charged on his allegiance to "deal no further with the Scottish cause," and so badly disgraced that he could find no one willing to be seen dining with him. Close to a nervous breakdown, he fled from court without permission and had to face what had been lurking in the background from the start — treason.

What followed was a study in desperation and maladroit timing. In November Norfolk, quivering with indecision, did

nothing; in December and January the Earls of Northumberland and Westmorland and Lord Leonard Darce of the North,
goaded on by their womenfolk, stumbled into ill-timed baronial rebellion and were resoundingly defeated; a plot to unseat
Cecil never got off the ground; cautious Philip of Spain ignored de Spes's sanguine reports that English Catholics were
ready by the thousands to die for Mary Stuart; and in February
the papacy in a staggering display of outmoded medieval concepts got around to liberating Englishmen from all "manner of
duty, fealty and obedience" to Elizabeth, just as some 750
Yorkshire peasants died on the gallows for their loyalty to a
feudal code that no longer had any meaning in Tudor England. Through no fault of her own, Gloriana triumphed, and
the succession question was left exactly as she wanted it: un-
resolved. Norfolk received a bad scare but not even his enemies
could prove overt treason, and Mary Stuart's stock plummeted
to a new low as moderates as well as Puritan radicals perceived
that the mere existence of that "mother of rebellion" was an
invitation to civil war.

A warning had been served: the wages of treason were
death. Alas, neither Mary nor Thomas Howard was capable of
learning the lesson. The Scottish Queen was too much a prisoner of her fairy-tale imagination and righteous indignation;
the Duke was too befuddled by a misplaced sense of immunity
conferred by his golden inheritance. By the summer of 1570
there was talk that both deserved death, and in 1571 they proceeded to hammer the nails into their respective coffins by becoming entangled in one of the most bizarre schemes to destroy
Elizabeth. The Ridolfi conspiracy took its name from as cheerful and criminally negligent a conspirator as ever plotted: Roberto Ridolfi, Florentine banker, confidant of kings, papal
courier and, more likely than not, Mr. Secretary's Cecil's secret
agent. Whatever his role — well-meaning but hopelessly in-

competent idealist who sought to rescue Mary and restore the old faith, or agent provocateur paid by Cecil to force Elizabeth's hand — the results could not have been better designed to destroy both Norfolk and Mary. In its final improbable form 6,000 Spanish troops were to land at Portsmouth and be joined by 39,000 fervent and armed Catholics; they were then to march on London where Norfolk would seize the Queen, rescue Mary, marry her, and reintroduce the Catholic faith. What was to become of Elizabeth was left in studied vagueness, but nobody had the least doubt what her fate would be. To such a scheme Mary and Norfolk lent their names. The Duke paid with his life, and there is no question that the Scottish Queen survived only because her English cousin had given her royal word.

The Ridolfi plot came to a boil during the spring and summer of 1571, and in late August the government, with the aid of thumbscrew and rack, uncovered a particularly unsavory mess of treason. Damning evidence was discovered in Norfolk's house, and even more incriminating letters were traced to Mary's secretary, the Bishop of Ross. Whatever else the Duke may have had in mind, it was undeniable that he had broken his promise to his sovereign never again to meddle in the affairs of Mary Stuart. In September he was bundled off to the Tower, and Sir Francis Knollys's warning came true: if the Duke sought to marry royalty "the realm must either destroy him or he destroy us." On January 16, 1572, he was unanimously found guilty of high treason by a jury of his peers. Elizabeth now had to make up her mind what to do with her Howard and Stuart relatives. In law Norfolk was already a dead man, and her original reaction to his treason was to have him executed out of hand. She had no mercy for those who touched her sceptre, but to send Thomas Howard to the block required her signature, and head chopping was one of those

irrevocable decisions which Elizabeth liked least. Moreover he
was her cousin, and to violate the claims of blood was to risk
the fate of Somerset, who had died twenty years before in part
because he had sanctioned his own brother's execution.

More baffling by far was what was to be done with that
"handmaid of iniquity," Mary Stuart. There could no longer
be talk of her restoration. Even the Queen had to admit that
Mary's thirst for the English throne was too insatiable to risk
setting her free, let alone restoring her crown. Elizabeth Tudor
was caught on the horns of a peculiarly personal dilemma
which placed the most treasured principles of her political life
in conflict: What should a sovereign do when legitimacy and
survival dictated diametrically opposite responses to a rightful
heir who was repeatedly conspiring to usurp her throne? The
Council had a perfectly statesmanlike solution: convene Parliament, pass a bill of attainder and execute "the daughter of
sedition." Gloriana, however, was far from convinced that
Parliament could legally resolve the riddle of a deposed but
nevertheless anointed sovereign who had commited treason in
a foreign realm. So she procrastinated, eventually bending to
the mounting pressure to summon Parliament in the self-
deceiving expectation that Lords and Commons might somehow make her mind up for her.

Parliament met on 8 May, 1572, specifically to devise legislation to protect the Queen's life and throne from the likes of
Norfolk. Officially there was no mention of Mary, but in every
mind was the determination to rectify the error that "there
was a person in this land whom no law could touch." Commons quickly left their mistress in little doubt as to where
they thought the source of the trouble lay. The causes were
twofold: the existence of popery throughout the kingdom and
the lack of an announced succession, which attracted every
kind of traitor to Mary Stuart's cause like so many bees to a

honeypot. The remedy was straight out of John Knox — strike at the roots lest "the branches that appear to be broke will bud again." Cut off the heads of both the Queen of Scots and the Duke of Norfolk, designate a successor to the throne, and debar the Stuart line. Neither Duke nor Queen deserved mercy. Submissions, subscriptions, oaths and protestations had not served to keep Norfolk loyal; it would be an ill example indeed and an invitation to further treason should he now escape his just deserts. As for Mary, sheer necessity dictated her death. She was indisputably "a queen's daughter," but what was this compared to the safety of their own sovereign who was "a king's daughter"?

Two inseparable issues — the royal prerogative and the divinity of kings — were at stake if Parliament dared order a queen to execute a sister sovereign. Reluctantly the House formulated two possible bills, one of attainder and execution, the other simply of exclusion from the succession. Elizabeth's response was predictable. In no uncertain terms she informed the Lower House that she would not, "partly for honour, partly for conscience" but mostly for "causes to herself known," have anything to do with an act which involved the execution of her cousin, and she ordered them to proceed with the second bill and draw up an exclusion law. The House would have no such half-measures. Were they, asked Paul Wentworth, to have "an axe or an act," and together Lords and Commons petitioned the Queen to reverse her decision. This time they were determined to do their homework and anticipate every ploy and maneuver of their mistress's fertile mind and subtle logic. Spiritual lords were to marshal reasons of conscience, laymen to handle matters of practical politics, and lawyers were to deal with arguments of law. In each case the presentation was designed to strike Elizabeth where she was most vulnerable. "God," explained the prelates, "willeth his magistrates not to spare either brother or sister or son or daughter or wife or friend" if they sought to seduce the truth. Mary was the sink and puddle of "adultery, murder, conspiracy, treasons and blasphemies." Not only did Elizabeth endanger her own soul and those of her people by refusing the Lord's manifest wish but she also failed in her royal function. She was sharply reminded that to be a king she must act like a king. Those worthy if bloodthirsty ecclesiastics had the Queen's father clearly in mind when they concluded that "the prince in government must be like unto God himself, who is not only amiable by mercy, but terrible also by justice."

The lay argument was more pragmatic and more telling: "desperation feareth no laws." Gloriana, however, remained unconvinced, and on May 28 she presented a deputation from Parliament with a thumbnail version of her lifetime policy. She was, she said, "resolved to defer but not reject" the attainder bill, and she wished them to go forward with the second act. The rejection was sugar-coated with layers of Elizabeth's most artful and affectionate prose, and Parliament chose submission to confrontation. Thwarted of Mary's blood, however, Commons demanded Thomas Howard's, and partly to avoid having to refuse still another petition, Elizabeth gave in. She had been dithering for weeks, having signed the Duke's death warrant back in February, then canceling it the next day. In gloomy disgust Cecil wrote to Walsingham that he had given up trying to penetrate the "inward cause" of her procrastination. One moment she spoke of "her danger" and judged that "justice should be done," the next she remembered "his nearness of blood" and refused to act; and Mr. Secretary was reduced to his usual conclusion: "God's will be fulfilled and aid her Majesty to do herself good." Fulfillment came on June 2, 1572. It was typical of Elizabeth, as of her father, that she refused to accept the responsibility for Norfolk's death and ever after blamed Cecil for having persuaded her to do what she knew was wrong.

The Queen should have accused Mary, not her Principal Secretary, for it was to save her Scottish cousin that she sacrificed her English Duke. Parliament had been doing its best with the exclusion bill, and in early June agreed upon a law that deprived the Scottish Queen of everything save her head. Mary was declared incapable of succeeding to the throne and, should Elizabeth die and Mary seek to reassert her title, the punishment was death. It was even judged treason if unbeknownst to her others sought to further her claims. The act neatly hamstrung Mary, but it had two serious drawbacks. From the Puritan point of view, by depriving Mary of her rights, Parliament was tacitly admitting the existence of a legal claim which the radicals absolutely denied. From Elizabeth's perspective the bill was tantamount to a lynch law, and during the debate only Mr. Francis Alford dared to point this out. Mary Stuart, he said, was as despicable a "creature as ever the earth bare," but it was repugnant to "the honour of England" to "condemn her unheard or to touch her in life for that which she never knew of," and he told the story of the monarch who had ordained the death of a fellow sovereign for treason and had then hanged the executioner so that "he should not vaunt himself to have been the spiller of so much noble blood."

Elizabeth agreed; no law could legally execute a divine-right king. Murder itself did not repel her, and she had her own solution for Mary Stuart: send her back a prisoner to Scotland with a firm guarantee from the Regent to have her quickly dispatched on Scottish soil. The ethics were right — survival justifies all — but the price was wrong. The Regent wanted three thousand English troops and the money Elizabeth had been spending annually to maintain Mary before he was willing to have murder done. The English Queen was covetous of her purse and reputation, and she feared that the presence of English troops would proclaim her own complicity and cost her foreign friends as well as money. So there was nothing to do but defy her subjects and save what Peter Wentworth indignantly referred to as "the most notorious whore in all the world." Parliament was prorogued on June 30, and through the Lord Keeper Gloriana informed her loyal Lords and Commons that she would take the bill under advisement. She tried to soften the blow by pretending that they were to take the term "advisement" literally, a suspension of judgment, but everybody knew it was a pocket veto, and not even "old Saturnus" Cecil could contain his anger at two months of negotiation, persuasion and headache postponed out of existence. "I cannot write patiently," he burst out to Walsingham. "All that we have laboured for . . . neither assented to nor rejected but deferred. . . ." Manfully he accepted the blame but his heart was so overthrown that he wearied of life itself. As always Gloriana had got her way; nothing had been resolved, all had been deferred, and Mary Stuart lived on, a trifling price to pay in the eyes of a Queen who had preserved her principles and kept her word of honor.

SEVEN

Neither Hot nor Cold

At the beginning it was but a cap, a surplice and a tippet; now it is grown to bishops, archbishops, and cathedral churches, to the overthrow of the established order. . . .

— DEAN OF YORK, *1573*

ALMOST A GENERATION before Elizabeth ascended the throne one of her father's bishops, John Skip of Hertford, wrote to an ardent and youthful religious scholar by the name of Mathew Parker; his letter revealed not only the difference in their ages but also the fundamental gulf between their concepts of what religion and society were all about. "Ye be hot and hasty," the tired Prelate wrote, "we be cold and tardy. We think that a great quantity of our qualities would do much amongst you, and a little of your qualities were enough for us." It was, he concluded, the differences in their approach that induced them to "proceed diversely." Eighteen years later Mathew Parker was Archbishop of Canterbury and the shoe was on the other foot. Now he had cause to brand eager young radicals as "precise folk" who "would offer their goods and bodies to prison rather than they should relent." After a decade of enforcing the settlement of 1559, Parker's words to his friend and colleague Mr. Secretary Cecil would have warmed the cockles of Skip's administrative heart: "Execution, execution, execution of laws and orders must be the first and last part of good government."

In 1559 Mathew Parker was in his mid-fifties; Elizabeth was less than half that age, but in matters of religion the Queen was old beyond her years, and she and her Archbishop, who had once been her mother's chaplain, shared a common approach to the church. Religion for both of them was essentially a formula for living and getting along upon an imperfect earth. Both were convinced that social discipline administered from above was a far surer imperative for right doing than the highly intuitive dictates of a regenerated heart open to God's grace and glowing with inward zeal. Parker was a most reluctant prelate, but like Cecil he suited his Queen perfectly. Doctrinally he was a product of her father's church: staunchly antipapal and aggressively English in his historic view of the church, willing to live with a comfortable degree of theological confusion, and, though disagreeing with Elizabeth over clerical marriages and her preference for papal trimmings, believing with all his heart in the royal supremacy. For Parker, as for the Supreme Governor, the settlement of 1559 was authoritative and final; Gloriana would continue her church and "leave it behind her" exactly as she had "found it at her first coming in." Mathew Parker voiced her feelings when he answered that difficult Puritan, Peter Wentworth, who suggested in 1571 that the reason all Romanist ceremonies had not been abolished back in 1559 was that there had been "no time to examine them, how they agreed with the word of God." "What!" the Archbishop sternly replied, "surely you mistook the matter. You will refer yourselves wholly to us therein." Wentworth, however, had the last word. His retort forecast the defiant mood of Puritans who, as the chosen vessels of God's purpose, knew themselves to be the equal of any earthly prince. "No," he told Parker, "by the faith I bear to God! We will pass nothing before we understand what it is, for that were but to make you popes."

Wentworth's appeal was not to reason, authority or expediency, but to that inward light which transcends logic and claims that nothing in life has meaning outside the spiritual drama of salvation and damnation, for when the cause belongs to God all else is "trifles in comparison." "Call ye them never so great," said one Puritan M.P., "subsidies, crowns, kingdoms," they are nothing in the face of the perfect rule that should be applied to every facet of life — "seek ye first the kingdom of God, and all things shall be added unto you." Here was the root of the religious controversy that set zealous souls apart from men of more pragmatic color.

Faith that could not be contained, that had to be translated into action and shared with all mankind, recognized no denominational barriers. In the sixteenth century it was the common if dangerous possession of both Catholic and Protestant, but during the first two decades of Elizabeth's reign it was the Puritan more than the Catholic who struck out against the "lethargy of the soul." What distinguished the Puritan from his Protestant brethren was the intensity of his faith, the logic of his approach which made it impossible for him to live with theological contradictions, the clinical interest he took in his soul's health, and the sense of rebirth and conversion which placed him among the spiritual elite and compelled him to hold both church and state up to the mirror of biblical perfection. Above all else Puritans were activists who bore the guilt of the world upon their shoulders. They imagined their own salvation was at stake unless they saved their brother Christians from damnation, and they felt obliged to labor in God's vineyard though they knew that good works could in no way change their predestined fate. It was sufficient simply to take an active part on the winning side. Puritanism appealed particularly to the enthusiastic busybody: "To bewail the distresses of God's children, it is puritanism. To reprove a man for swearing, it is puritanism. To banish an adulterer out of the house, it is puritanism. To make humble suit to her Majesty and the High Court of Parliament for a learned ministry, it is puritanism." "The Lord," one good Puritan exclaimed, "send her Majesty store of such Puritans."

Elizabeth wanted no part of God's store of Puritans. In her eyes they were dangerous egotists and spiritual hypochondriacs, making too many subtle scannings" of God's blessed word, and she bluntly informed them that she would not "tolerate new-fangledness." Gloriana may have had her moments of religious doubt and could write in the dark of the night — "What have I rendered to Thee? Forgetfulness, unthankfulness and great disobedience. . . . I should have prayed unto Thee; I have forgotten Thee. I should have served Thee; I have sinned against Thee. This is my case; then where is my hope?" — but during the day she had nothing but contempt for the sick souls of this world, and she ordered her bishops to "look unto such men" who "of late have said that I was of no religion — neither hot nor cold, but such a one as one day would give God the vomit."

The Queen's quarrel with her Puritans went to the root of her personality and revealed her for what she was — not only her father's daughter but in an important sense the last of the medievalists. Her views on society and the proper relationship between church and state were closer to Cardinal Wolsey and the tradition of the great ecclesiastical statesmen of the past than to the theocratic notions of John Calvin or Peter Wentworth. Ever since the break with Rome, church and state had been ruled by a common head, but the essential duality of medieval society remained: two parallel and complementary institutions endowed with authority over men, and ordained by God as the twin swords of Christ. Order still existed in "ruling and obeying," and Elizabeth "as a mother over her children" made it perfectly clear that she would countenance no rival power in either church or state. The "caterpillars of the commonwealth" took many forms. Some tried to grow fat upon the foliage of the state, and like Norfolk and his baronial colleagues in the northern shires had to be destroyed before they could eat away the roots of all good government — the divine authority of the crown. Others like the Puritans struck at religion, which was in the Queen's words "the ground on which all other matters ought to take root, and being corrupted may mar all the tree." They were "overbold with God Almighty" and sought to remodel the church according to their own fancies. Elizabeth had no need of the Spanish Ambassador's advice "to look at the intentions which these people, professing the new religion, display; their only effort being to disregard their superiors," or his pointed reference to "bear in mind the obedience and quietude of the Catholics compared with the turbulence of the Protestants." Puritans were nothing but trouble, and when she told the Ambassador that she did not know "what the devils wanted," she got the succinct answer she knew to be true: "liberty."

The vitality of fervent souls had once been blunted or absorbed in the monastery; now the Wentworths of Elizabethan society sat in Commons, brazenly informing their Queen that they would "regard no manner of person," for Parliament must be a place "to glorify God and benefit the Commonwealth." In many ways the dynamism and self-confidence of Gloriana's England grew out of this intense concern with translating

God's will into daily life. In their several ways Puritans, pioneers and profiteers were all in a hurry; each sought "new worlds for gold, for praise, for glory." Such men were unwilling to wait upon history or authority and were careless of the very elements the Queen most cherished — tradition, priority and place. The ultimate irony of Elizabeth's reign was that the greatness of her century rested in large measure upon the restless energy and passionate loyalty of exactly those people she most disliked and mistrusted. As far as she could she threw her entire weight against their activities, and she regarded the Puritan as more dangerous to the Tudor state than any northern earl. Elizabeth was quite right, but for once time and fortune were only temporarily on her side. She won all the battles, but in the end the Puritan spirit would triumph in both church and state. What she achieved was a holding action which helped create the miracle of Elizabethan England, that fragile, ephemeral balance between the static, introspective and organic medieval past and the mobile, extroverted and individualistic future.

The first clash between the Queen and God's elect came early in the reign and arose from flattering but excessive Puritan concern for Gloriana's safety. For every Protestant the glaring fault of the settlement of 1559 was twofold: first, it had not demanded the death penalty for those Marian clerics who had refused the Oath of Supremacy, and second, it allowed a multitude of Catholics to hide behind the theological confusion of the Prayer Book and the ridiculously light penalty of a single shilling imposed upon those who failed to attend the established church. All but 189 of 9,000 clergy had taken the Oath of Supremacy, but Protestants had cause to suspect that the majority were still practicing their idolatrous religion. Surely it was time to enforce the Thirty-Nine Articles, which contained the creed of the Anglican church and had been agreed upon by Convocation in 1563, time to purge the church of sloth, expel the crypto-Catholics and require the godly to stand up and be counted.

Elizabeth did not believe, any more than anyone else in the mid-sixteenth century, in the principle of toleration, but she knew from firsthand experience the futility of "making anatomies of hearts" either to reveal true loyalty or to detect secret malice. Again and again she avowed that she demanded of her subjects only their personal, almost feudal, loyalty to herself as Queen and, "in their outward conversation," to show themselves to be "quiet and conformable and not manifestly repugnant and obstinate to the laws of the realm." She had no wish that the "maintainers of false religion . . . die by the sword," and in the spring of 1563 when Parliament overwhelmingly passed legislation imposing the death penalty on all who twice refused the Oath of Supremacy, she circumvented the bill by ordering Archbishop Parker not to demand the oath from the Marian prelates for a second time except on her written command. She fully agreed with Robert Atkinson's exhortation to the bloodthirsty in Commons: "Since you have the sword in your hand to strike, be well aware whom you strike. For some shall you strike that are your near friends, some your kinsmen, but all your countrymen, and even Christians."

It was relatively easy for a Supreme Governor to refuse to enforce parliamentary statutes, but from the moment Mary Stuart arrived in England it was exceedingly difficult to answer the argument, offered by moderates and radicals alike, that a kingdom surrounded by enemies without could not countenance a variety of faith within. As ideological war approached, the Puritan cup of frustration brimmed over. Why did the Queen persist in chastising her loyal and godfearing subjects with popish regalia, the devil's livery, yet wink at Catholic monstrosities practiced by would-be traitors? Why could she not perceive that if her kingdom were "linked together in the fear of God and in true concord and amity among ourselves . . . no enemy, no foreign power can hurt us"? When Parliament was called in April of 1571 to pay the exorbitant cost of suppressing treason and Catholicism in the north, the cry went up that only through reform and conformity could the realm ever achieve unity and English souls and purses be safeguarded against "both corporeal and spiritual enemies." Bishop Sandys of London set the tone in his opening sermon to Parliament. "One God, one king, one faith, one profession is fit for one Monarchy and Commonwealth. . . . Let conformity and unity in religion be provided for; and it shall be as a wall of defense unto this realm."

The Bishop's logic was faultless — all agreed that division was weakness, concord strength — but Elizabeth and her Parliament immediately fell out over whether unity involved conformity of souls as well as bodies. In the teeth of their mistress's disapproval both houses pushed through legislation compelling the clergy to subscribe to the Thirty-Nine Articles, requiring all subjects to attend church, and imposing a crushing hundred-mark fine on any Catholic who failed to take Anglican communion at least once a year. It was one thing to exorcise secret Catholicism in the name of national defense, by insisting that the clergy subscribe to the official creed of the English church and by requiring all good Christians to attend church, but quite another to demand that every subject take communion. Such a requirement was in defiance of the Queen's public promise given "in the word of a Prince and the presence of God" not to molest her subjects by way of "inquisition of their opinions for their consciences." Though Elizabeth stood alone, at odds with Cecil, her Council, Parliament and the overwhelming body of Protestant opinion, be it Anglican or Puritan, there could be no going back upon a monarch's word, and she did not hesitate to veto bills so distasteful to her rooted convictions. Nevertheless, as cold war turned to hot, she could find no defense against the Puritan position that "not only the external and outward show is to be sought, but the very secrets of the heart in God's cause . . . must come to a reckoning, and the good seed so sifted from the cockle that the one may be known from the other." Reluctantly the Queen retreated, and during the 1580s and 1590s sanctioned ferocious legislation designed to destroy Catholicism, root and branch.

In the face of political necessity Elizabeth could be depended upon to give in, but on the issue of the finality of her religious settlement of 1559 she was adamant. During the Parliament of 1571–1572 Puritans had played a double game, demanding conformity for their enemies and freedom of religious thought for themselves. Throughout the next two decades they extended their attack, striking at the historic and divine roots of the ecclesiastical polity, its episcopal structure, its spiritual foundations and even at the royal supremacy itself. They sought to legislate the new Jerusalem in their own image, thus challenging the Queen's prerogative and destroying the divinely ordained society that she had inherited from her father, where subjects obeyed their betters without "presumption" and lived "quietly and charitably together, each one in his vocation." Invariably the attack was heavily veiled in decorous and loyal phrases, but there was no mistaking the threat to Tudor absolutism when God directly inspired Peter Wentworth and gave him courage to speak his mind. By 1576 the time had come to use God's rod and make proud episcopal "buttocks to smart," and on the first day of parliamentary business Wentworth rose. "Two things," he said, "do very great hurt" to freedom of speech. "The one is a rumour" that "the Queen's Majesty liketh not of such a matter"; the other that a royal "message is brought into the House, either of commanding or inhibiting" discussion. Having struck at the heart of the Queen's control, her right to initiate legislation and to guide debate, Wentworth proceeded to compound his crimes by direct criticism of Gloriana herself. Elizabeth had sinned grievously in her handling of Parliament; she had refused to bind herself to the wishes of her "most loving and faithful nobility and people," and in doing so had encouraged the "hollow hearts" of her hateful enemies. Only when God was served would there be good legislation, and he concluded by announcing to his astonished colleagues that "we are incorporated into this place to serve God and all England, and not to be time-servers and humour-feeders."

Though Peter Wentworth's defense of freedom of speech was not, as he feared, to "be buried in the pit of oblivion and so no good come thereof," and would be remembered by future generations who would topple the Tudor paternalistic state on exactly this point, the initial impact of his words was to shock even his most ardent admirers and to bring down upon him the wrath of his sovereign. Men who speak for God, however, cannot be repentant, and he boldly told a committee of the House appointed to question him that he was not ashamed of what he had said and would gladly say it again. "Yea," said his interrogators, "but you might have uttered it in better terms. Why did you not so?" The answer revealed the abyss between ideological revolutionists and defenders of the established order. "Would you have me to have done as you of her Majesty's Privy Council do? To utter a weighty matter in such terms as she should not have understood to have made a fault? Then it would have done her Majesty no good, and my intent was to do her good."

Puritans continually complained that their Queen misjudged them, and old Sir Francis Knollys marveled that "her Majesty can be persuaded that she is in as much danger of such as are called Puritans, as she is of the Papists." Even after a lifetime of observing his mistress in action Sir Francis was blind to what made Puritans so abhorrent in Elizabeth's eyes: their pride in their own humility. It might be expected that the vehement Mr. Peter Wentworth would dare to criticize God's anointed lieutenant on earth and say that "none is without fault: no, not our noble Queen," for "her Majesty hath committed great faults — yea, dangerous faults to herself and the State." But the spirit of obsequious rebellion was on the march when the modest and retiring Archbishop Grindal, appointed by the Queen herself to follow in Parker's administrative footsteps, turned on his sovereign and wrote: "Bear with me, I beseech you, Madam, if I choose rather to offend your earthly majesty than to offend the heavenly majesty of God. . . . Remember Madam, that you are a mortal creature . . . and although you are a mighty Prince, yet remember that He which dwelleth in Heaven is mightier."

Elizabeth never denied her mortality or the limitations of her earthly majesty, accounting herself no better than God's "handmaid," but the conditions of her alliance with the Almighty were hers alone and were not to be trumpeted from every pulpit, let alone questioned by a servant of her own church and of her own creation. Grindal's reminder was not only tactless, it struck at the bedrock upon which her supremacy rested — her divine authority in matters of church organization and discipline. She repudiated, she said, "any superiority in ourself to define, decide or determine any article" of the faith, and she sought no windows into the secret reservations that might lie hidden within her subjects' souls, but she was adamant in maintaining her authority as God's vicar to order her people "to live in faith," and to "see the laws of God and man which are ordained to that end to be duly observed." An archbishop could not possibly serve two masters, and when

Grindal hesitated to outlaw Puritan conclaves for spiritual self-criticism on the grounds that Elizabeth had no right to say "as I wish, so I command; take my will for reason," Gloriana was understandably indignant. She did not, as legend has it, write the disobedient Bishop of Ely, "Proud Prelate, you know what you were before I made you what you are. If you do not immediately comply with my request, I will unfrock you, by God!" but she did inform her bishops that "if you, my Lords of the clergy, do not amend" your ways "I mean to depose you: look ye therefore well to your charges"; and only the strenuous opposition of Cecil and her Council prevented her from relieving Grindal of his spiritual office. She did, however, have the satisfaction of depriving him of his administrative authority and placing him under house arrest.

Living as she did in the midst of endless intrigue, it is understandable if the Queen was attracted by the conspiracy theory of history and believed that Puritans aimed at the overthrow of the state as well as the church. The very logic of their creed seemed to demand it, and Elizabeth went to the root of the matter when she told the Puritans in the Commons of 1584–1585 that it accorded ill with her concept of royal authority "to have every man, according to his own censure, to make a doom of the validity and privity of his Prince's government, with a common veil and cover of God's word, whose followers must not be judged but by private men's exposition. God defend you from such a ruler that so evil will guide you." A decade later she was even more convinced of the case. Her last and most sympathetic Archbishop of Canterbury, John Whitgift, had warned her that those "who seek to bring in a new kind of ecclesiastical government, like unto that in Scotland, and do, as far as they dare, impugn your Majesty's authority in causes ecclesiastical . . . [will] endeavour also to impair the temporal" jurisdiction and "bring even kings and princes under their censure." Monarchs had to stand together in defense of their species, and the aging Queen had no hesitation in warning her youthful brother of Scotland "that there is risen, both in your realm and mine, a sect of perilous consequence such as would have no kings but a presbytery. . . . Yea, look we well unto them. When they have made in our people's hearts a doubt of our religion, and that we err if they say so, what perilous issue this may make I rather think than mind to write. . . ." Long before James coined the bon mot "no bishop no king," it was commonplace in Elizabeth's England to rhyme:

> Yes, he that now saith, "Why should bishops be?"
> Will next cry out, "Why Kings? the saints are free."

History was to prove the worth of Bess's judgment, but during her reign she did her saints an injustice. They were not free; they were bound to her by chains of sheer necessity. While Mary Stuart lived and Jesuit "hellhounds" preached armed and "pestilent conspiracy against the Church of God," Puritans were willing to delude themselves into believing that evil councillors, not the Queen, were responsible for godless legislation. In an orgy of misguided innocence one of the brothers-in-Christ told his parliamentary colleagues that there were ministers "about her Highness as not only will not inform her" of the errors and abuses rampant within her church "but also do keep from her gracious sight" Puritan efforts to reform the house of God. "Without all doubts," he assured his naïve listeners, if her Majesty would only be truthfully informed of their saintly purpose, "she could not, considering her zeal towards the building of the Lord's house, but with all speed cut off those abuses" and rebuild according to sound Puritan architectural plans. Such was the triumph of hope over experience! Extraordinary as it seems, Puritans continued to wish their

Queen well despite the overwhelming evidence that their sovereign lady was temperamentally, historically and politically opposed to everything they held most dear.

Puritan self-deception and the Queen's magnetism were soon put to the test. Elizabeth had understood perfectly the implications of Peter Wentworth's words on free speech, and at the close of the Parliament of 1576 she rose without warning to deliver a carefully phrased oration filled with elusiveness and captivating remembrances. She started with a whopping disclaimer that cried out for denial. "If I should say the sweetest speech with the eloquentest tongue that ever was in man, I were not able to express that restless care which I have ever bent to govern for the greatest wealth." She confessed herself, as well she might, to be baffled by her own success and by the love that subjects were so eager to bestow upon her. "Whereas variety and love of change is ever so rife in servants towards their masters, children towards their parents, and in private friends one towards another . . . yet still I find that assured zeal amongst my faithful subjects, to my very special comfort. . . . How great my fortune is in this respect, I were ingrate if I should not acknowledge." The credit, she said, belonged not to her own devices but to God alone, "the Prince of rule." With this bow to the Lord, however, Elizabeth was quite ready to list the benefits that had occurred during her administration, and she asked her people to remember "the bitter storms and troubles of your neighbours." The moral was clear, and doubtless she had Wentworth in mind when she said: "Let all men therefore bear their private faults: mine own have weight enough for me to answer for." She made no direct mention of Wentworth's defiance, but said that she too was a devotee of God's truth and that all her life she had placed service to the Lord above convenience, policy and worldly riches. It was an exceptional performance and Elizabeth was justly proud of it.

Between the Queen's tender touch and Wentworth's over-strong medicine no more was heard of Puritan reform for a time — a very short time. What the Puritans could not achieve in Commons, they endeavored to bring about outside of Parliament, aiming at "a discipline in a discipline, presbytery in episcopacy." Elizabeth's answer was to renew her own brand of discipline. In September of 1583 Archbishop Grindal died and was replaced by John Whitgift, a man who so suited the Queen that he was known in Puritan circles as "her black husband." He at once devised a threefold religious test to which the clergy had to subscribe: belief in the supremacy, acceptance of all Thirty-Nine Articles, and acknowledgment that the Prayer Book in no way contravened the word of God. The disciplinary powers of the ecclesiastical Court of High Commission were increased and doubtful ministers were interrogated under oath. It all savoured of the Inquisition, and Cecil sharply criticized the Archbishop's methods as rather a "device to seek for offenders than to reform any." Elizabeth was going on fifty and her rule was hardening. Flexible and chameleonlike in so much that she did, in religious discipline she grew more and more rigid, and now demanded of her Puritans not only outward obedience to the settlement of 1559 but also open approval of its doctrines — something she had never required of her Catholics. Suddenly the Thirty-Nine Articles, which the radicals had wanted to use as a religious test to weed out secret Catholicism, were being directed against themselves. Here indeed seemed to be proof that both the rod that chastised them and the episcopal institution that wielded it were godless in the eyes of the Lord and must be destroyed.

Twice more — in 1584–1585 and 1586–1587 — Puritans turned to Parliament in their effort to legalize what was rapidly becoming revolution, and both times they were befuddled and paralyzed by the opiate of the Queen's gracious words and stern refusals. Knowing full well the vulnerability of legislation at the hands of a sovereign with the right of veto, the Puritans tried to conceal their rebellious purpose in the guise of a humble petition delivered to the spiritual and temporal peers, asking that pastors evicted by Whitgift be restored, that those who failed to conform to every article of the church not be persecuted, and that unlearned ministers be removed and replaced by candidates approved by the parish congregations. Little wonder the Archbishop complained that the petition "smelleth of popular election," and that Elizabeth removed the velvet glove. In no uncertain terms she ordered the Speaker to inform his rebellious House that she knew herself to be "Supreme Governor of this Church, next unto God." He was instructed to warn them to "forbear any further proceedings," for she would "receive no notion of innovation, nor alter or change any law whereby the religion or Church of England standeth established at this day." Let them, she said, take their grievances to the bishops if they desired the redress of abuses.

Rarely was Gloriana so brutally direct; rarely did she elect so blatantly to hide behind the Speaker in dispensing her chastisements, and as a consequence she stirred up a hornet's nest in Parliament. The House, in defense of its liberties, criticized the Speaker for delivering such a message and defied the Queen by promptly incorporating many of their grievances into statutes, the most unacceptable being a bill to remove clerical appointments from episcopal control and deliver them into lay hands. The saints did not get their bills, but it was a near thing, and at the close of the session Elizabeth was forced once again to use her trump card: the magic of her personality and the impact of her oratory. She set out as always to beguile her audience. "No prince herein, I confess, can be surer tied or faster bound than I am with the link of your good will." Then she turned to her purpose; "one matter toucheth me so near, as I may not overskip; religion." If there be faults "with the order of the clergy," then she would see to it that the spiritual lords looked to their charges and rectified the disorder on pain of deposition. For herself, few had read more deeply or had sought to follow God more diligently, "and so you see that you wrong me too much, if any such there be as doubt my coldness in that behalf." Hers was the true way of God; otherwise she would never have presumed to "prescribe it to you."

Elizabeth might have saved her breath; God's elect found the Queen's prescription totally unpalatable, and when Parliament next met in October of 1586 the moment of truth seemed to be at hand. Religious hysteria was in the air; Protestant England stood alone, beleaguered by the regiments of Catholic Spain abroad and by papal fifth columnists at home. If true believers were ever to be forged into a Calvinistic army of elected soldiers, now was the appointed time. Book, bill and buckler would inaugurate the new and triumphant society: a book of prayer conceived in the purity of Geneva and in "the light of God's glorious gospel"; a bill to wipe clean the filth of generations, cast out all "laws, customs, statutes, ordinances and constitutions," including even the Act of Supremacy, and substitute a presbyterian order of government; and a buckler of total spiritual conformity to shield the Queen and her kingdom from "the fury of Spain, or the treachery of France, or the hosts of the Assyrians, or all the power of Hell and darkness."

Anthony Coke gave his name to Bill and Book, and both were introduced into the Lower House in February of 1587, the one to be enacted into law, the other to be read and pondered. There was, however, no godly legislation or contemplation of divine truth, for Elizabeth promptly commandeered both Bill and Book. This time Commons was prepared, and Peter Wentworth was ready with a set of explosive questions: "Whether it be not . . . against the law that the Prince or

Privy Council should send for any Member . . . and check, blame, or punish them for any speech used in this place, except it be for traitorous words? . . . Whether it be not against the . . . liberties of this House to receive messages either of commanding or prohibiting . . . [or] to make anything known unto the Prince that is here in hand. . . ." Almost within the hour the redoubtable Wentworth got his answer; he was clapped in the Tower. Next day Coke and the other ringleaders followed him, and before the session was finished Elizabeth sent a harsh message to her errant Puritans. "Her Majesty hath fully considered" all the criticisms "and doth find them frivolous" and "most prejudicial to the religion established, to her crown, to her government, and to her subjects." Two years later she was even more outspoken. Her Majesty was "most fully and firmly settled in her conscience, by the word of God, that the estate and government of this Church of England, as now it standeth in this reformation, may justly be compared to any church which has been established in any Christian kingdom since the Apostles' times; that both in form and doctrine it is agreeable with the Scriptures, with the most ancient general Councils, with the practice of the primitive church, and with the judgments of all the old and learned fathers." The subject was closed; no one was henceforth to "meddle with any such matters or causes of religion, except it be to bridle all those, whether Papists or Puritans, which are herewithal discontented."

It deeply disturbed the brothers-in-Christ to hear their Queen lump godly Puritans and hateful papists together, but time and circumstance, as well as their Supreme Governor, deprived them of resistance. As their mistress said, she considered "it very inconvenient and dangerous, whilst our enemies are labouring to overthrow the religion established, as false and erroneous, that we by new disputations should seem ourselves to doubt thereof." Not even "the godly brotherhood" was willing to risk outright revolution when the Beast stood at the door. Gloriana may have needed her difficult Puritans, their insatiable energy and happy conviction that God was English, but they also needed their Queen lest God's citadel, imperfect as it was, be altogether destroyed. The ramparts held and Elizabeth's enemies were everywhere confounded, but a price was paid. Puritanism, at least for Elizabeth's reign, was sacrificed upon the altar of national survival. By the time the crisis of the Armada had receded, the brotherhood was so split by rival factions that the Queen and "her dark husband" had little difficulty in muzzling the Puritan spirit and, as in so much else, ordering time to stand and wait upon the arrival of the luckless James I.

EIGHT

Sometime So, Sometime No

God direct the matter for I have done my uttermost
and so hath other Councillors here.
— LORD BURGHLEY TO WALSINGHAM, 1572

What it shall please her Majesty to do is in the hands
of God.
— THE EARL OF SUSSEX to WALSINGHAM, 1578

"YOU PURITAN! You will never be content till you drive me into
a war on all sides and bring the King of Spain on to me!" The
Queen's anger was directed at Sir Francis Walsingham in February of 1581, eight years after he had joined her Council as
one of the two Principal Secretaries of state. Both the accusation and prediction were substantially correct. Thwarted in
their drive to build the ark of the Lord's Covenant at home,
Sir Francis and his brothers-in-Christ were determined to advance God's glory in foreign parts and cast their princess as the
defender of a particularly expansionistic brand of Calvinism.
Puritans had their way but not exactly as they would have
liked it. War with Catholic Spain came before the decade was
out, but Elizabeth declined the role of Protestant champion

and adamantly refused to change the base and bumbling principles of her foreign policy.

Diplomacy, marriage treaty and war: together they consumed most of her working hours and represent the bulk of what remains of the documentation of her reign, but no one, then or now, has ever been quite sure what actually underlay all this activity. Did it conceal personal spite, imperfect understanding, unwarranted optimism and pathological inability to decide between alternative courses of action? Or was it the product of the calculated application of flexible and subtle means to limited but attainable ends? The case can be made either way. Her ministers, though wise and flattering after the event, during the actual course of an international crisis were reduced to helpless fury and fervent prayer by a mistress who was "sometime so, sometime no, and all times uncertain and ready to stays and revocation." Walsingham was the most outspoken of the Queen's councillors, and during the carnival of marital negotiations between England and France in 1581 he wrote Cecil from Paris giving open vent to his frustration with a sovereign lady who would not or could not make up her mind. "I would to God her Majesty would resolve one way or the other touching the matter of her marriage. . . . When her Majesty is pressed to marry then she seemeth to affect a [diplomatic] league and when a league is yielded to, then she liketh better of a marriage. And when thereupon she is moved to assent to marriage then she hath recourse to the league, when the motion for a league or any request is made for money, then her Majesty returneth to the marriage." A decision had to be made, and he begged the Council to "move her Majesty to grow to some earnest resolution in that behalf." Cecil's tired response concluded with the pessimistic words, "What may further move her Majesty hereafter I know not, but I see it common to great and small not to think of adversity in time of prosperity and so adversity cometh with double peril."

Historians, knowing the outcome of Gloriana's mercurial tactics and capricious policies, have used hindsight to see beyond the halting and contradictory methods to the skillful plotting beneath. It has been argued that what appears to be vacillation was in reality careful preparation for all eventualities, a strategic design to defend the kingdom from attack by neutralizing, not conquering, those areas from whence an invasion might be staged: Scotland, the Netherlands and France. In a general sense this may be true. Elizabeth's diplomacy had a simple and sustained purpose — the defense of the realm and the preservation of her throne, her faith and her majesty — but to state the proposition is, in fact, to say very little. Walsingham and Cecil had the same broad patriotic goals, but they conceived their ends in far more positive and activistic terms, and their means were so different from the Queen's that at times they doubted whether their sovereign had any other purpose than to throw dust in their eyes and wait upon events.

In contrast to their mistress, both men knew exactly what they wanted, and they knew how to achieve it in terms of the realities of sixteenth-century international politics. From the start the Renaissance state, at best a fragile contrivance of the bureaucratic mind and secular spirit, had been at the mercy of feudal violence, provincial loyalties and administrative ineptitude. The infant leviathan, preserved only by scaffold, stake and statutes written in blood by strong-willed princes, was ill prepared to withstand the onslaught of religious war in which earthly loyalties were cast aside for a higher fidelity. The spirit of martyrdom was everywhere on the increase, and in horror and disgust Thomas Digges, Puritan by conviction, mathematician by training and rationalist by instinct, noted that "against persons so persuaded, no peril of death, no horror of punishment or torments can prevail. They desire the one, they triumph in the other." Such fanaticism touched the hearts of both Catholics and Protestants and produced throughout Europe a rash of political assassinations, committed on the moral grounds that if kings "do ill and be wicked, they must be dealt withal." If the Queen was to survive, it seemed clear to Walsingham and Cecil that not only must she take extreme precautions against the assassin's blade, noxious perfumes and balls of deadly incense, but also she should take advantage of the new spirit of the age: Christians were "ready, one to cut another's throat for matters of religion."

National defense for both men involved far more than the immediate welfare of God's Englishmen. It encompassed ideological conflict between Christ and Antichrist, good and evil, which was predicated upon a vision of the future that included all Europe. Walsingham was more militant, committed and crusading; Cecil more pragmatic, cautious and skeptical; but both saw clearly that the stoutest defense was a strong offense, and that neighbors composed of brothers-in-God meant policies favorable to England. They differed only in degree and application. Cecil was insular: the kingdom's salvation involved continued intervention and support of the Protestant party in Scotland; Walsingham was a Europeanist, arguing that the Queen's safety lay in a divided continent, and urging her to foster civil and religious war in France and the Netherlands for the avowed purpose of teaching proud Philip of Spain "what it is to serve against God." What both men could not comprehend, but had to learn to work with, was their sovereign lady's egocentric response to the affairs of Europe.

The Renaissance prince had not yet coined the expression *l'état, c'est moi*, but Elizabeth persisted in viewing foreign affairs from the special perspective of her royal office. The defense and inviolability of kingship, far more than her own personal security or even the protection of her kingdom, was the central theme of her policy, for by definition what was good for royalty was good for her subjects. "In all your doings," one political analyst advised his Queen, "remember the majesty of your person, wherein consisteth the politique life of all your people," and "the health of your state and theirs." If the principle was sound for domestic consumption, it should apply also to international relations which were, after all, simply the rules by which monarchs lived and warred with one another. Christendom, though torn by rival ideologies, was still for old-fashioned people like Elizabeth a community of sovereigns held together by the common divinity of their persons and the common good of their estates. There might be, indeed there always had been, conflicts between kings, but these, as in her father's day, were wars which did not "bitterly wound" the hearts of princes, for they were fought within the system of the divine right of kings and not between competing concepts of divinity. The word of a prince still counted, as did the obligations of treaties even when they appeared to contravene the advancement of God's glory. When French Catholics butchered thousands of Huguenots on St. Bartholomew's Day, 1570, and Charles IX maintained his innocence, claiming that he had been stampeded into action for fear of a Protestant plot against his authority, not his religion, Elizabeth at least in public was inclined to believe him, just as she persisted in giving Mary Stuart the benefit of the doubt when she denied conspiring against the English throne. Whatever the truth, factual or divine, it was necessary to maintain princely standards, and all her life Elizabeth firmly believed in appearances.

As a member of a European association of monarchs, it was every sovereign's obligation to support the lawful authority of fellow kings, for what monarch could sleep secure in his bed if his neighbor were giving his subjects lessons in sedition. Philip, in disciplining his "incontinent, ungrateful" Dutch subjects, was doing, as Cecil dryly commented, "a thing that any prince would do, and as her Majesty did upon the like occasion both in England and in Ireland." Elizabeth believed in the established order of things and had no desire to change the world into which she had been born. Instead she sought to return to what had been, to put the clock back to the days of her father and to restore legitimate government. Only in desperation and when Philip himself had breached the principles of princely conduct by laying claim to her throne, enforcing the papal bull of excommunication and overtly supporting her Irish rebels, did she permit open intervention in the Lowlands, and even then she was "tempted greatly both to repent herself of aiding them and to attempt how to be quit of them."

Committed to the status quo, Elizabeth tended simply to react to change and never, if possible, to instigate it. Like Leicester, Walsingham and Cecil she desired her own safety and that of her kingdom, but these were absolute ends in themselves and never conceived as means to some future goal. The loss of Calais would continue to rankle but the port was part of the past, not of the future; it belonged to England by historic right, not military might. For the rest of the continent and even Scotland, she was satisfied with the power structure which she had inherited in 1558, and she did not fully appreciate the forces of change that were ripping apart the diplomatic fabric of the past. She never looked to the New World to rectify the balance of the old, and when in 1580 Sir Francis Drake returned from his circumnavigation of the globe to a hero's welcome, Gloriana was more impressed by his cargo of East Indian cloves and his profits of 4,700 percent than by the new Albion of California which he had claimed in her name. Like her father she saw Europe as the focal point of English interests. She never forgot "that old league that had lasted long between the race of Burgundy" and her progenitors, and she failed to realize that the traditional links holding England and the Low-lands had corroded since the days when Philip the Good and Charles the Bold had ruled by the grace of God, and the entire economic prosperity of England had been geared to the Ant-werp wool trade. During Elizabeth's reign wool was no longer king; other European outlets were being developed to handle English trade, and the cosmopolitan but militarily weak dukes of Burgundy had been replaced by Philip of Spain, the most powerful prince in Christendom. Spain, not France, was the colossus of the continent, yet Elizabeth could not forget that the Valois were the historic enemies of her land. Her final decision to help Philip's Dutch subjects was actually made as much from fear that France would intervene and gobble up the Netherlands as from any desire to chastise her aggressive brother-in-law.

Elizabeth's policy never fitted Cecil's tidy and rational sum-maries of the pros and cons of diplomatic action or Walsing-ham's crusading fervor, because it consisted largely in reacting to events and deciding on immediate remedies. It was a pedes-trian and parochial approach based on idiosyncratic principles of legitimacy, history and divinity which her Council never fully understood. Generally it had more to do with the state of her exchequer than with the state of Europe, for if Elizabeth was old-fashioned in her perception of the diplomatic scene, she was starkly modern in her realization that money was power. By any financial reckoning England was a second-rate kingdom, yet it was being asked to subsidize James of Scotland, preserve the independence of the Lowlands, finance the new Bourbon monarchy of France and take on the Spanish giant.

Under the circumstances it is understandable that Elizabeth refused to subscribe to the opinion that "sparing and war have no affinity together."

Given her objectives, Elizabeth's methods made considerable sense. She invariably preferred inaction to action, diplomacy to war, half-measures to full measures and prevarication to truth, so long as diplomatic appearances could be maintained, the cost minimized and her opponents prevented from taking extreme countermeasures. Her instinct was always to hesitate, delay and hope for the best, in the optimistic conviction that by doing little or nothing she was safeguarding herself from doing the wrong thing. When action could not be avoided or when it was forced upon her, she preferred underhand means, hiding behind subterfuge, diplomatic smokescreens and the letter of the law. Again and again she was accused of deceitfulness and hypocrisy, and even an old campaigner like Cecil begged her to drop her backstairs and parsimonious support of James of Scotland and to come out openly in defense of what was so obviously to England's advantage. It was, he said, a profitless course and far more dangerous than outright intervention. Walsingham had much the same advice for the Lowlands, but Elizabeth had three excellent reasons for her secrecy and half-measures: money was saved, the fiction of legitimacy and legality was maintained, and policy was kept out of the hands of the military, over whom Gloriana realized she had almost no control.

It is a cliché to say that Queen Bess loved peace, not war. Certainly she liked to pose as the goddess of mediation and moderation, and she informed the Spanish Ambassador that she wished to "God that each had his own and all were content." Nevertheless the statistics belie the legend. Her reign opened and ended in war; she ordered the invasion of Scotland and France within three years of coming to the throne; she maintained an English army on the continent for almost twenty years; she sent more troops into Ireland and spent more money on the conquest of that graveyard of English reputations than any of her predecessors; and though it is difficult to distinguish between hot and cold, public and private war, the kingdom was in open conflict with Spain for nearly half the reign. It is not enough to say that the last forty years of the sixteenth century was an era of prolonged, intermittent and brutal civil and international war into which England was swept willy-nilly. There is no evidence that Elizabeth had a rooted aversion to organized killing if it served her purpose. What she objected to was the unpredictable and costly nature of war. It was a ferocious monster to feed; as often as not it resolved nothing or produced unexpected consequences; and most frustrating of all, it placed her in the hands of military leaders who ignored her instructions and did exactly as they pleased the moment they left her presence.

Nothing revealed the Queen's "sexly weakness" as did armed conflict, and nothing infuriated her more than the footless and heroic prancing of her warriors. When Leicester led his troops into the Lowlands and against her explicit orders assumed the title of Governor-General, she launched one of her sharpest invectives against a well-behaved court favorite who had become a disobedient and swaggering soldier the minute he was placed in charge of troops: "Jesus! What availeth wit when it fails the owner at greatest need! Do that you are bidden and leave your considerations to your own affairs. . . . I am utterly at squares with this childish dealing." Four years later, when her youthful Essex ran off to join Drake's attack on Spain in 1589, she sent off a shower of letters ordering his immediate return. Sir Francis as the commanding officer calmly ignored her wishes, and not until she had grimly commanded him "as we have authority to rule, so we look to be obeyed" did the old sea dog ship the Queen's errant Earl back to court to face the fury of a sovereign lady who had just written: "Essex . . . we gave directions to some of our Privy Council to let you know our express pleasure for your immediate repair hither; which you have not performed. . . . We do therefore charge and command you forthwith . . . all excuses and delays set apart, to make your present and immediate repair unto us. . . . Whereof see you fail not, as you be loath to incur our indignation, and will answer for the contrary at your uttermost peril." Essex returned, but two years later he was gallivanting about France at the head of a tiny expeditionary force, challenging the governor of Rouen to single combat to decide whether "my Mistress is more beautiful than yours." Since his mistress had just told him not "for respect of any vain glory, to put in danger your own person," the Queen was understandably vexed, and scornfully dismissed his escapade as "rather a jest than a victory."

Elizabeth had excellent reasons to suspect that her admirals and generals "went to places more for profit than for service," which explains why, as Raleigh complained, she preferred scribes to men of war. Francis Bacon sensed that under the exterior of princely rule she was in fact a little frightened of the military, and he warned Essex that his constant boasting about being a soldier might cause alarm in a lady "of her Majesty's apprehension." Elizabeth liked her soldiers for show, as window-dressing to the ritualistic and structured life she lived. Only when her "men of high mettle" were without the means of war, like chimneys in summer, did she feel safe in the knowledge that her authority was complete. This, of course, entailed as few military and as many diplomatic adventures as possible.

Elizabeth delighted in diplomacy, for it kept control firmly in her hands and lent itself to what she did best — nuances, innuendos, verbal displays and the endless thrust and parry of negotiations in which everybody knew the precise rules of the game. Her chosen weapon was marriage. Unscrupulously and with great personal satisfaction she offered her virginity to the highest bidder. Since she never fulfilled her promises and probably never intended to do so, she must be accounted more a tease than a prostitute. The fulcrum upon which her foreign policy rested was the absolute upset in the balance of power occasioned by the internal collapse of France and the emergence of Spain as the arbiter of Europe. Philip's responsibilities were many and his administrative and military burdens were legion, but God rewarded his efforts and protected his far-flung possessions on which the sun never set. Only in the economic jewel of his empire, the seventeen prosperous provinces of the Lowlands, did the forces of sedition and heresy make headway. The Dutch provinces had been in open revolt since 1566–1567 when endemic distaste for Spanish taxes, fear of the Catholic Inquisition and dislike of a foreign master who ruled a thousand miles away in the isolation of the Escorial had been fanned into outright rebellion by Calvinist fanaticism and militancy. Philip had responded first with butchery and suppression under the Duke of Alva and then with moderation and restraint under his bastard brother Don Juan, but treason and heresy had continued to prosper. When he asked the reason, he invariably received the same answer: "The only remedy for the disorders of the Netherlands is that England should be ruled by someone devoted to your Majesty." The explanation was simplistic, more an excuse for Spanish incompetence than a realistic analysis of the situation, but it added a particularly heinous grievance to Philip's long list of complaints about his English sister-in-law.

During the first decade of the reign Elizabeth had operated on the happy assumption that no matter what the provocation Philip would always prefer English Elizabeth to French Mary

Stuart on the throne. The King of Spain had indeed been so preoccupied in the Mediterranean that he had had no choice but to ignore the potential danger of a Protestant citadel threatening his Catholic lifeline to the Lowlands. By 1568, however, it was clear that a reckoning was not far off. English merchants — Philip preferred to call them pirates — had been poaching on Spanish mercantile preserves for years, and in September of 1568 Messrs. John Hawkins and Francis Drake paid the price. In a spectacular display of Spanish treachery or, depending on who is telling the story, of sensible response to brigandage and heresy, their fleet was surprised and destroyed in the Mexican harbor of San Juan de Ulva. Elizabeth's revenge came two months later, when she commandeered a shipment of Spanish gold destined for Alva's troops in the Netherlands. The two kingdoms approached the brink of war, then backed away, for Philip and Elizabeth had one quality in common: they disliked irrevocable decisions and preferred diplomacy to war. As Cecil commented, "I cannot think it convenient either for the King of Spain or for us to bring this unkindness to a flat falling out."

There was no falling out but there was a diplomatic revolution. Fear of Spain brought a hiatus to one of the most ancient and cherished enmities of early modern Europe. In April of 1572, by the Treaty of Blois, England and France patched up their differences and promised to come to one another's aid if attacked by a third party. A precarious friendship with an old and inveterate enemy, however, was too uncertain a reed upon which to stake a showdown with Spain. Conciliation seemed the better part of valor on the part of a Queen who had to match Spain's dazzling riches with an ordinary income that never kept abreast of the inflation, and a grudging parliamentary contribution that was rarely enough. From 1572 on Elizabeth was determined to give Philip no further cause for complaint, and she closed English ports to Dutch pirates, although she somewhat marred the effect by failing to interfere with the flow of volunteers and private money pouring across the Channel. The Queen was "very melancholy" and "out of quiet." It was all very well to condemn rebellion in principle and piously to pray for a mediated peace which would restore the ancient liberties of the Burgundian provinces but, as her Council was at pains to point out, if she did nothing to help the insurgents they would be defeated and the resources of the Lowlands directed against England. As long as Dutch resistance under William of Orange was reasonably successful her solution as usual was to equivocate. She gave the Dutch Estates £20,000, promised a loan of £100,000, and against the passionate advice of her ministers offered England's good services in negotiating a peace between the rebels and their rightful governor. The only consolation Cecil could offer Walsingham was to "wish you patience," for he knew the grief of spending long hours only "to find so small fruits." Walsingham answered "how unpleasant it is to be employed in so unfortunate service I leave to your Lordship's judgment."

In the end circumstance forced Elizabeth's hand. Neither Philip nor the Dutch Calvinists wanted peace on any terms except their own, and in 1577 the youngest of Catherine de' Medici's sons, big-nosed, pock-marked yet incurably romantic, Francis Duke of Alençon, began to intrigue in the troubled waters of the Lowlands in the hope of winning himself a crown. Elizabeth immediately smelled French intervention and hoisted her matrimonial sails, intimating that she regarded Alençon, aged twenty-two, ripe for her mature charms of forty-five. For the next four years Gloriana was in her element, tempting the impecunious Frenchman with money and marriage whenever she perceived signs of independence of action, but rebuffing his ardent courtship whenever her suitor's strained relations with his brother and mother seemed to minimize the possibility of active French support in the Netherlands. It was all as intricate and dangerous a courtship as any two scorpions contrived, and Elizabeth very nearly got badly stung. Emotionally she was at her most vulnerable; she was going through menopause and this was her last serious matrimonial fling. Moreover, faithful Leicester had deeply hurt her by secretly marrying the despicable Lettice Knollys, and most embarrassing of all, Alençon kept fulfilling all of the conditions for marriage imposed upon him, even agreeing to come to England for inspection. She was, she said, "between Scylla and Charybdis. Alençon has agreed to all the terms I sent him and he is asking me to tell him when I want him to come and marry me. If I do not marry him, I do not know whether he will remain friendly with me; and if I do, I shall not be able to govern the country with the freedom and security I have hitherto enjoyed." Eventually Elizabeth had to decide; as Cecil said, "Words were no satisfaction but that deeds must do it." When the Duke arrived in England during the spring of 1581, the Spanish Ambassador was willing to take a hundred to one odds that there would be no wedding, and he was right — virginity prevailed. Alençon tore off the ring Elizabeth had given him, complained that she had made him the laughingstock of Europe and that English women were as fickle as their climate, and burst into tears. By way of consolation the Queen gave him a handkerchief, £10,000 in cash and a promise of £50,000 more.

It was just as well that Elizabeth did not couple herself with the engaging Frenchman. Three years later at the age of thirty he was dead of a lung infection; and the following month, July of 1584, William of Orange followed him to the grave, murdered by a Catholic cabinetmaker's apprentice who was determined to demonstrate that no one was too lowly to strike a

blow on God's behalf. Alençon's death paved the way for dynastic war in France and ended any possibility of French help
in the Lowlands. William's death and the military and diplomatic skills of Alexander Farnese, Duke of Parma, very nearly
ended the Dutch revolt, and confronted Elizabeth with exactly
the decision she had been so studiously avoiding: whether to
provide armed support to Calvinists and rebels. Cecil pondered
the pros and cons of intervention in one of his exquisitely balanced and deceptively dispassionate presentations, which allowed his mistress to pluck off the arguments as if they were so
many petals on a daisy — to intervene or not to intervene. The
final decision belonged to Elizabeth, and she took refuge in haggling over terms; the Dutch must yield the ports of Brille and
Flushing, in return she might be able to manage 4,000 foot
soldiers, 400 horsemen and £4,500 a month, but she expected
to "be repaid to the last farthing" when the war was over, and
under no circumstances would she assume responsibility for
the rebellious provinces, let alone accept their proffered sovereignty. Then there was the problem of the commander: Leicester or someone else, for Gloriana had not yet forgiven her
Robin for his faithlessness in marrying Lettice Knollys. While
Elizabeth bargained, Parma completed the encirclement of
Antwerp, and in desperation on August 12, 1585, Elizabeth
committed herself to a war that could have but one conclusion
— a showdown with Spain.

Stark military necessity dictated the final decision, which
involved troops and monies far in excess of Elizabeth's original
offer to the Dutch, but by the late summer of 1585 the Queen's
conscience was nowhere near as tender as it had once been, for
her brother-in-law had twice proved himself to be a false
prince. Philip had broken the rules of kingly behavior in sub-
sidizing Catholic chieftains in Ireland, and in March of 1580
Elizabeth bluntly told Mendoza, the Spanish Ambassador, that

if his master did not stop she would "let out" in the Lowlands: Two could play at the same game. Three years later not even Elizabeth could ignore the ugly truth that legitimacy as an effective principle of international relations was meaningless in the midst of ideological war, for in 1583 Philip proved that the word of a prince meant nothing when dealing with a heretic. Confronted with a disastrous failure of the Spanish wheat crop, he begged English merchants to send relief; when they did, he confiscated every last ship and boasted that he would use the vessels in his Great Enterprise to punish that "incestuous bastard" and "shame of womanhood," Bess of England. It is difficult to say whether at any time armed conflict with Spain was inevitable. Left to their own tortoiselike devices, Elizabeth and Philip might have done nothing for so long that an entirely new combination of occurrences might have developed which would have precluded war, but by 1581 events were locked into such a fixed pattern of aggression and reprisal that all decisions were conditioned by the expectation that war was inevitable.

When Elizabeth sent Alençon packing and the safety of the kingdom could no longer be secured by means of a dynastic alliance, Cecil immediately raised an issue to which he was quite sure he knew the answer, for it had been on his mind for over thirty years: "Should war break out" English Catholics will listen rather to what they will consider the voice of God, calling on them to restore the papacy, than to the voice of the King calling on them to obey." There was real cause for alarm. For almost a decade Catholic missionaries, smuggled into the country by the dozens, had been teaching the downtrodden and disheartened that neither God nor the pope had forsaken them and that retribution would soon be at hand. Rome had proclaimed that whoever helped rid the world of Elizabeth would be a public benefactor, and in the spring of 1583 it was rumored that the Duke of Guise was ready to add silver to religious merit if anyone would liquidate such "a serpent and a viper." Throughout 1583 the government was aware of the existence of a complicated international system of espionage and conspiracy reaching from Scotland to Antwerp, Rome and Madrid, and centered upon the "hope of all idolatry," Mary Stuart. With the help of the rack Mr. Secretary Walsingham, that "most subtle searcher of secrets," discovered in November an ambitious plot to rescue Mary, restore Catholicism and expose the realm to the military rule of the Duke of Parma. There was evidence that Bernardino de Mendoza was directly implicated, and he was summarily given fifteen days to remove himself from the kingdom. He left as unrepentant and ill-informed as ever, and harshly reminded Elizabeth that though he had failed "as a minister of peace" he would try to "satisfy her in war."

Mendoza was gone, but to the disgust of all good Protestants the real culprit, Mary Stuart, remained. In an outburst of righteous indignation loyal subjects throughout the realm set their hands to the Bond of Association, a secret vigilante society sworn to destroy not only the perpetrator of the Queen's death but also all persons for whose benefit the assassin acted. The Association was an ugly sign of religious bigotry, born and nourished by the repeated plots to kill Elizabeth and by the successful murder of William of Orange, and Gloriana would have nothing to do with it. It was patently aimed at Mary Stuart, and the Queen made it clear that she would not have the divinity of kings set aside in the name of public vengeance. In the eyes of her Council, however, Mary remained the center of infection. As long as "the Scottish lady" lived every disloyal heart contained the seed of hope. Only in her death could the nightmare of Catholic insurrection be dispelled and Protestants sleep at ease. Since Elizabeth would not allow them to

resolve their fears with the ax, the Council introduced into
Parliament legislation designed to safeguard the Queen's life
by guaranteeing that should the Scottish whore ever again be
implicated in treason and be found guilty, no amount of divinity could save her from execution. The question was whether
such an act would serve as a deterrent. Sir Francis Walsingham
thought not, and he set about proving that Charles IX had
spoken the truth back in 1571 when he had said of his sister-
in-law, "The poor fool will never cease until she lose her
head. . . ."

Left with nothing but her faith and her dreams, Mary spent
endless hours composing impassioned but impractical letters to
anyone who would give the time to read them, and depicting
in exquisite needlework the cat and mouse game carried on
between two of the most resourceful and determined women
in Europe. During the summer of 1586 the Stuart mouse took
the bait and the Tudor cat jumped. Mary Stuart could not
resist giving her blessing to the ill-conceived schemes of Anthony Babington and six other well-placed gentlemen, who
promised to undertake the "trajical execution" of Elizabeth.
Again with the aid of Parma's overworked troops Mary was to
be delivered from her enemies and the true faith reinstated
throughout the land. This time, however, she put her approval
in writing, and in so doing she signed her death warrant. For
months Mary's correspondence had been inspected, her ciphers
decoded and her channels to the outside world riddled with
double agents, all for a single purpose: to glean the evidence
that would bring Mary of Scotland under the Act for the
Safety of the Queen and to force Elizabeth to commence legal
proceedings against her cousin.

Both ladies ran true to form. Elizabeth could not make up
her mind even to place Mary under stricter surveillance, let
alone appoint a commission to try a divine-right queen for

treason, and in a rare outburst of exasperation Cecil wrote Walsingham that "we are still in long arguments but no conclusions do last, being as variable as the weather." The Tower was too sinister, Hertford Castle too close by, Fotheringhay too far, and every other suggestion not "allowed." "And so, ever with weariness by talk, her Majesty hath left all off till a time I know not." Eventually Fotheringhay was chosen and the trial began on October 11. Mary was at her maddening and marvelous best, blandly dismissing the evidence with a smile, warning her judges to "remember that the theatre of the world is wider than thé realm of England," and protesting "as an absolute Queen" that she could not "submit to the laws of the land without injury to myself, the King my son and all other sovereign princes. . . ." For Cecil and the rest of the commissioners the argument was rubbish; Mary had long since forfeited her claim to royal immunity, and she was without a shadow of doubt "an imaginer and compasser of her Majesty's destruction"; but Elizabeth, though she did not deny the evidence and would not reverse the verdict, could not accept the logic that her safety required "a Princess's head." There yet remained that inviolable community of sovereigns. "What will they not now say," she asked, "when it shall be spread that for the safety of her life a maiden Queen could be content to spill the blood even of her own kinswoman?"

Only Gloriana who was directly responsible to God had doubts. For everyone else the decision was self-evident: Mary was a "wicked and filthy woman" who thirsted after the crown, "a murderer of her husband," and a "detestable traitor" whose "villainy hath stained the earth and infected the air." Her death would be "one of the fairest riddances that ever the church of God had," and on November 12, 1586, without a dissenting voice both houses of Parliament petitioned the Queen to proceed according to the law, to have the judgment of the commission published and the warrant of execution signed. Elizabeth answered from the throne in honeyed words that "drew tears from many eyes" but as usual said nothing, promising only "with earnest prayer to beseech His Divine Majesty so to illuminate mine understanding and inspire me with His grace, as I may do and determine that which shall serve to the establishment of His Church, preservation of your estates, and prosperity of this Commonwealth under my charge." Twelve days later she informed them what God had inspired. She began with a confession: "I have strived more this day than ever in my life whether I should speak or use silence. If I speak and not complain, I shall dissemble; if I hold my peace, your labour taken were full vain." She continued with a barefaced lie — "For me to make moan were strange and rare" — but she rectified the balance by pointing out a simple and courageous truth: "I am not so void of judgment as not to see mine own peril; nor yet so ignorant as not to know it were in nature a foolish course to cherish a sword to cut mine own throat; nor so careless as not to weigh that my life daily is in hazard." Yet she proposed to do nothing about it, asking her subjects to "rather marvel that I am, than muse that I should not be if it were not God's holy hand that continueth me beyond all other expectations." She then concluded with the understatement of the reign: "So have I not used over-sudden resolutions in matters that have touched me full near: you will say that with me, I think." As for the petition, "Your judgment I condemn not, neither do I mistake your reasons, but pray you to accept my thankfulness, excuse my doubtfulness, and take in good part my answer-answerless. . . . Therefore, if I should say, I would not do what you request, it might peradventure be more than I thought; and to say I would do it, might perhaps breed peril of that you labour to preserve, being more than in your wisdoms and discretions would seem convenient, circumstances of place and time being duly considered." It was a masterpiece of procrastination and vagueness, displaying the volatile qualities of her mind and her exquisite mastery of prose, but it fooled no one, and Cecil caustically commented that men would soon be calling "this a vain Parliament, or otherwise nickname it a Parliament of Words."

Elizabeth, as she said, was not "so void of judgment" as to be totally blind to "her own peril," and despite her words she had in fact made up her mind — Mary must die. What caused the anguish and the sleepless nights was not so much the shedding of her cousin's blood as the manner of her execution. The Queen dropped hint after hint that others should ease "her of this burden" and privately dispatch Mary by poison or suffocation, but she could not permit raison d'état to be sanctioned by law; it led straight to Charles I. She could live with her private conscience that countenanced killing in self-defense, but not with her public reputation should it permit the violation of the divinity of kings. Both Mary and Elizabeth agreed that personal monarchy had its own morality; common folk might call it hypocrisy and indeed Mary's keeper, Sir Amyas Paulet, declined to "make so foul a shipwreck of my conscience" as to "shed blood without law and warrant," but as the Queen knew, he was hiding his conscience behind her signature. She realized that not only was the responsibility hers but also that appearances and style were crucial to kingship; had she not said, "We Princes . . . are set on stages, in the sight and view of all the world duly observed. . . . It behoveth us, therefore, to be careful that our proceedings be just and honourable." It was scarcely honorable "that she, of all Christian princes, should be the first author of so strange a precedent" as to legally execute a sovereign who could not be judged except by God.

It took Elizabeth two months to inch her way to the violation of the most sacred principle of sixteenth-century monarchy. On December 1 she permitted Cecil to publish the proclamation of Mary's sentence; later that month he was allowed to draw up the warrant of execution; on February 1 she signed it and ordered Secretary William Davison to have it recorded by the Lord Chancellor; the next day she began to backtrack and asked "What needeth that haste?" Davison, suspecting that he was being groomed as a scapegoat, sensibly rushed to Sir Christopher Hatton for advice. On the third the full Council, secretly convened at Cecil's house, agreed that the Queen should not be allowed to fall "into any new conceit of interrupting or staying the course of justice." The Council assumed collective responsibility for sending the warrant on to Fotheringhay for execution, and every member swore to keep the decision secret from the Queen.

At ten o'clock on Wednesday the eighth of February Mary Stuart died as she had lived, conscious to the last that she was "descended from the blood of Henry VII, a married Queen of France, and the anointed Queen of Scotland." Her cousin of England wept and stormed when she was told the news and swore that she had never intended that the warrant should be executed; then she wept again when none could be found who quite believed her. In her fury and remorse she had poor Davison committed to the Tower and swore that on her own authority she would have him hanged as a Judas. Cecil was banished from court, and for the next month she was in such a foul mood that Walsingham confessed that "in dealing with her I am nothing gracious; and if her Majesty could be otherwise served I know I should not be used." Elizabeth might scold her Council for arrogantly contravening her will and acting behind her back, but she could no more do without Cecil than without Walsingham, and by May he was back in the "broil," sadly assuring his sovereign that he was ready "to wear out the

short and weak thread of my old, painful and irksome days as
your Majesty shall limit them. . . ."

Mary's execution brought war with Spain one step nearer,
for Elizabeth had added the murder of God's anointed to her
sins. The courts of kings cried out, at least in public, for vengeance, but only Philip was willing to act; Henry III of France
cared for nothing except his own pleasures and James VI of
Scotland was said to have whispered on hearing of his mother's
death — "Now I am sole King." Revenge spurred Philip on,
but in fact the decision to administer the judgment of heaven
upon the English Jezebel had been taken years before. Both
sides saw the forthcoming ordeal as the fulfillment of God's
will. "The Lord hath vowed himself to be English" was for
Gloriana's subjects a simple statement of the truth. For His
Most Catholic Majesty of Spain the outcome was equally certain. He calmly wrote to Medina Sidonia, the man whom he
had placed in charge of his Great Enterprise and who was well
aware of both his own inadequacies as a sailor and the naviga-
tional and logistical hazards of sending one hundred and thirty
vessels into English waters: "If you fail, you fail, but the cause
being the cause of God, you will not fail. Take heart and sail
as soon as possible."

Philip's great galleons, displaying on their banners the stir-
ring words "Arise, O Lord, and vindicate Thy cause," sailed
up the Channel in August of 1588 only to be smashed by a
combination of wind, tide and Elizabeth's beardless boys. If
the defeat of the Armada Catholique proves anything, it indi-
cates once again that God helps those who help themselves.
The previous year Elizabeth had been persuaded to send
twenty-three ships "to impeach the purpose of the Spanish
fleet" and Drake had scuttled sixty-five vessels that had been
fitting out in Cadiz harbor. He had then swept on, looting the

coastal trade and burning the seasoned barrel stays designed for the wine and water kegs of Philip's fighting ships. As a consequence, when the Armada finally sailed, its barrels were of green wood and the flight north around Scotland and Ireland was turned into an agony of thirst and suffering, for most of the wine and water had leaked away. Drake's heroic marauding may have played a role in the ultimate destruction of the Armada, but technology, not valor, won the battle. Spanish galleons, medieval relics built as platforms for pikemen and musketeers, were ungainly floating castles; they were met by a new kind of warship and a new concept of naval warfare, in which fast, maneuverable vessels destroyed one another with high-caliber guns that could turn the four-foot-thick sides of any galleon into a death trap of twisted timbers and flying splinters. After it was all over and some fourscore dying vessels out of a fleet of one hunded and thirty crawled home in defeat, Spanish historians found solace in the knowledge that the Armada had been vanquished not so much by the guns of heretics as "by the elements, against which valour and human daring are impotent because it is God who rules the seas." But the Lord did more than send Protestant cold and tempest: He sent the Armada upon an impossible mission. Medina Sidonia's instructions were to avoid battle, rendezvous with the Duke of Parma and escort his troops in the invasion of England, but Philip controlled no deepwater port where his oceangoing galleons could join with Parma's troop carriers and horse barges. Again Elizabeth was unimaginably lucky in the messianic blindness of her opponent. As Raleigh later said, "For to invade by sea upon a perilous coast, being neither in possession of any port, nor succoured by any party, may better fit a prince presuming on his fortune than enriched with understanding." Philip did not realize that the Queen of England, not the King of Spain, was fortune's chosen child.

NINE

Good Mistress — Dread Sovereign

My good mistress is gone, I shall not hastily put forth
for a new master.
— JOHN HARINGTON, *Nugae Antiquae*

THE YEAR 1588 had begun with foreboding and dire prophecies
of "horrible alteration" and the overthrow of kings, but as the
grim statistics recording the fate of Medina Sidonia's fleet
came slowly in — two warships captured, three stranded on the
coast of Flanders, five destroyed by English cannon, eleven galleons and twelve troopships lost in the gray waters of the North
Sea or torn to pieces on the rock-strewn shores of Scotland and
Ireland, and possibly a dozen lesser vessels "fate unknown" —
it became apparent that once again providence had made an
exception for England's Eliza. "God," as one ecstatic observer
of the final decade of Gloriana's reign happily noted, "is not
changed. He hath said He will defend Queen Elizabeth, His
anointed servant that trusteth in Him, and He hath done it."
In their several ways, Elizabeth and her brother-in-law acknowledged the Lord's hand. Philip taciturnly commented

that "in God's actions reputation is neither lost nor gained: it is best not to talk of it." The Queen — astute showman that she was — sat for a new "Armada" portrait and ordered the royal mint to strike a silver medal commemorating the destruction of the Spanish fleet with the succinct words: "God breathed and they were scattered."

God had not changed but His anointed servant had — she was fifty-five. The fresh young girl of twenty-five who had inherited a faltering throne had imperceptibly given way to a stage production. The "Armada" portrait, designed for reproduction by the hundreds for the benefit of a self-satisfied, self-glorifying kingdom, enshrined not so much a woman as an icon, dazzling, timeless but lifeless. Gloriana stood still, but time crept by; the flesh withered, the nose sharpened, the teeth decayed; her beardless boys grew old, lame and gouty; and most grievous of all, a younger generation of Essexes and Raleighs, Bacons and Robert Cecils were beginning to sense that "overmuch . . . unwieldiness of state" was sapping the strength of Gloriana's monarchy, and were finding it increasingly embarrassing to live with an idol who survived on memories which grew more distant and unreal with each passing year.

Crudely, cruelly time transformed the Queen and her court into caricatures of their former selves. The court, which had been designed for kings and under Henry VIII had been enveloped in a locker room atmosphere — masculine, intimate and casual — became an extravagant and stylized stage where, said the Queen's godson, "there was no love, but that of the lusty god of gallantry, Asmodeus." More and more Bess relied on masquerade and deceit to achieve her effect. Cosmetics encroached upon nature; false hair and whalebone concealed reality; and ritual replaced the spontaneity of youth. Once Elizabeth had told the miniaturist Nicholas Hilliard that she

detested shadows and preferred clear, clean lines; now everything in life was harsh line, accentuating the worst, mocking
the best. The gallantry of Leicester at fifty-two was stilted but
sincere when he wrote his irate mistress that his sole comfort
was in "reposing evermore under the shadow of those blessed
beams that must yield the only nourishment" to his "wounded
heart." Christopher Hatton's delightfully extravagant but
metaphorically mixed compliments "upon the knees" of his
heart still sounded felicitous in the mouth of a bachelor who
alone of the Queen's swains remained single: "This is the
twelfth day since I saw the brightness of that Sun that giveth
light unto my sense and soul; I wax an amazed creature." But
Hatton and Leicester were of Elizabeth's generation. Similar
words rang false when written by the twenty-four-year-old
Earl of Essex to his bewigged and bepowdered sovereign.
"While your Majesty gives me leave to say I love you, my fortune is as my affection, unmatchable. If ever you deny me that
liberty, you may end my life, but never shake my constancy, for
were the sweetness of your nature turned into the greatest bitterness that could be, it is not in your power, as great a Queen
as you are, to make me love you less." Essex's constancy was
conditional, his affection purchasable, and within the decade
he had turned traitor.

As Elizabeth grew older she became increasingly difficult and
inflexible. Her "choler" and "ireful speeches" grew more fre-
quent, tongue lashing and ear boxing more common, and
lengthy sojourns in the Tower occurred more often for those
who violated her strict sense of decency and decorum. The
tragedy of Gloriana's final years was that she had been born
into a generation older than herself and had outlived her cultural contemporaries. Providence continued to bless her actions, but the gods did not play fair, for the essence of her
peculiar brand of success was that it was predicated upon time

and survival. She had survived and now had to pay the price of having buried all those worried, earnest souls who had warned her that life was short and hell an eternity, that she must name a successor or risk her soul, that she must secure her dynasty by wedlock and guard her life from the sinister plottings of Antichrist, and that action, decision and calculation were essential to sound policy. Dudley, her loyal Robin, died in November of 1588, conscientious Francis Walsingham was dead by the spring of 1590, and eighteen months later Christopher Hatton, her Bellweather, followed him to the grave. Then the pace quickened; in swift succession came the deaths of Drake and Hawkins, octogenarian Sir Francis Knollys, who had always thought it "a deadly grief . . . to offend her Majesty, especially publicly," and ancient Blanche Perry who could remember when she had rocked the Princess in her cradle. By 1598 only the original cast was left — old Saturnus Cecil whose single-hearted service had earned him the title of Lord Burghley, Philip of Spain alive but entombed in his palatial mausoleum, and Elizabeth who could still dance to tabor and pipe but who was more and more at odds with a generation whose morals she viewed as lax, whose antics she regarded as childish, and whose political and economic principles she saw as materialistic and dangerously "popular." If she scolded like a universal nanny she had cause. Essex insulted Charles Blount and challenged him to a duel simply because Elizabeth had presented him with a golden queen from her chess set; Lord Admiral Howard cut away Essex's signature with a knife because the young commander had placed his name before that of the Lord Admiral in their joint report to the Queen; Raleigh backed one of the uglier of the Queen's maids-of-honor "up against a tree" and got her pregnant; the Earls of Southampton and Pembroke did the same to Elizabeth Vernon and Mary Fitton; and Sir Walter as Captain of the Guards dressed his troops in orange and yellow plumes during the Ascension Day tournaments of 1598, but Essex stole his splendor by arriving with two thousand men all resplendent in identical plumage.

The Earl of Essex's military posturing was more than a juvenile masquerade; it was symptomatic of the mounting frustration that gilded youths felt for a government of old men grown "out of date," their zeal as withered as their brows. Deprived of real power, there was little else to do but strut and preen, quarrel and fornicate. The men who had taken control in 1558 had been a generational unit; the image of the Queen's father was vivid in their memories; so also was the recollection of the "outrageous frenzy" of Edward's and Mary's reigns. Their social habits were conservative, their political instincts old-fashioned, and Burghley for one saw no need to make concessions to young men willing to risk all that had been so painstakingly constructed for the sake of honor and military renown. Young hotheads, he concluded in 1593, "were quick, as martial men are most commonly," and he was "slow, as men in their years are . . ." but "her Majesty misliked not my slowness, whereby I am the better confirmed in my opinion." Throughout the nineties "slowness" prevailed. Burghley may, as Spencer caustically rhymed, have been "broad spreading like an aged tree [that] lets none shoot up that nigh him planted be," but it was the Queen herself who cast the longest shadow. The peculiar triumph of her reign had been her ability to satisfy every expectation with a smile. As the century advanced, however, and the spell faltered, more and more it was whispered that every man expected mountains but found only molehills, that it was easier to attain "the Kingdom of Heaven" than win a "pension or office to an earthly King," that "niggardness" triumphed everywhere, and that the court was "full of discontents and factions."

"When grey hairs grow silent, then young heads grow ven-
turous." Youth was turning away from the past with its senseless dread of discord and disarray, its endless prating about
"the sweetness of unity, the fatness and substance of religion
[and] the wine of obedience," and its hypocritical preaching
that "we should not look at what we cannot reach, nor long
for what we should not have. Things above us are not for us."
The Queen was old, crotchety and cantankerous; the established religion to which she clung was a collection of theological platitudes divorced from living faith or inner meaning; and
her court was a brittle charade as encrusted with ritual as old
Bess herself was "thick with jewels." Almost in defiance a
younger generation turned to war, the quest for honor, the
service of God, be He interpreted by Rome or Geneva, and
most serious of all to political doctrines that shattered the
magic of the Queen's mystique and were fatal to the divinity
that sustained her throne.

The potent memory of "Harry with the crown" who had
known himself to be a "god on earth" was fading into oblivion
when John Selden, who was a child of four when the Armada
set sail, could write that "a king is a thing men have made for
their own sakes, for quietness' sake. Just as in a family one man
is appointed to buy the meat." When royalty becomes a pur-
veyor of pork and beef and monarchs must dress themselves in
the drab clothing of utilitarianism, the days of Tudor absolutism were numbered, but it was arrogant, rebellious Essex who
voiced the creed that would one day unseat a host of kings. He
had quarreled violently with his sovereign, and with Elizabeth's
slap across his face and stinging rebuke still ringing in his ears,
he wrote in fury to Lord Keeper Egerton: "What, cannot
Princes err? Cannot subjects receive wrong? Is an earthly power
or authority infinite? Pardon me, pardon me, my good Lord, I
can never subscribe to these principles." The Earl may have

been indulging more in masculine egotism born of feudal pride and Renaissance conceit than in serious political analysis, but a new atmosphere was emerging, as one by one the Queen's contemporaries died, leaving Gloriana alone like some aging but magnetic Hollywood star who has outlived all her leading men. It would not be long before a later generation would look upon the stiff, two-dimensional portraits of those starched and ruffled heroes of a bygone age and comment: "Christ, what a fright."

In 1588–1589, a younger generation was ready and waiting, impatient to prove that "if there were any good thing to be done in these days, it is the young men that must do it." It was unimaginable that real power would be denied them for another decade, and for the time being at least they were satisfied to test their manhood in a triumphant war so obviously pleasing to God. Everyone was optimistic, for the "teeth and jaws of our mightiest and most malicious enemy" had been broken. Philip, despite his "terrible ostentation," had not "so much as sunk or taken one ship, bark, pinnace or cockboat of ours or even burned so much as one sheepcote of this land," and if further evidence of heavenly approval was required, all England recognized God's will when on August 1, 1589, a frenzied Dominican monk drove a knife into the unprotected belly of the last of the Valois kings. Divine intervention suddenly transformed Protestant Henry of Navarre into the Most Christian King of France, and with a great sigh of relief Elizabeth watched as the center of the struggle between Christ and Antichrist, Catholic and Protestant moved from the Netherlands and the English Channel to the gates of Paris.

For years Elizabeth had been bothered both in her conscience and her pocketbook by her aid to Philip's Dutch rebels; it was morally wrong and consequently profitless. Each year £160,000, three-fourths of her normal peacetime revenues, were being poured into a footless adventure in which English arms were conspicuously unsuccessful and only fat Amsterdam burghers contrived to earn a penny out of death and destruction. "By the living God" she swore she would have "nothing more to do with such people." Step by step the war effort in the Netherlands was scaled down while financial and military involvement on behalf of her brother sovereign, the rightful King of France, increased. For once principle and policy coincided; she was supporting legitimacy and at the same time thwarting her brother-in-law, whose Spanish armies were seeking to impose upon France a Hapsburg pretender — Philip's own daughter by his second wife, Elizabeth Valois.

Gloriana's interest in France was not solely concern with defending the divine right of Bourbon inheritance; she had not forgotten Calais. France in the death grip of religious madness might yet relinquish England's ancient continental foothold; and in 1596, when Spanish troops besieged the port, the occasion presented itself. Both Henry and Elizabeth were confronted with a knotty problem in international sophistry. Should Navarre ask for English assistance and thereby risk Calais being saved by an ally who might never give it back, or should he permit the port to fall to an enemy who might be depended upon to return it once a final peace had been signed? Should Elizabeth, without French guarantees that her troops would be permitted to stay, rush to the rescue of the town, thereby driving Navarre into the arms of Spain and chancing a repetition of the Newhaven fiasco, or should she stand by, hoping that the French garrison would be able to hold out and prevent Philip from seizing a deepwater port in which to harbor yet another armada? What transpired is evidence that hesitation and greed rarely mix well and that Elizabeth could misplay her hand. As usual she followed a delaying policy of her own devising which ignored the overwhelming opinion of her Council. The moment word arrived in late March that Calais was being besieged even Burghley urged his mistress to respond quickly, but Elizabeth refused to act. She saw a chance to recover English property by blackmailing Henry into giving a written promise that her troops would be welcome in the citadel of Calais itself, and could stay until he had repaid the £350,000 he owed her. On Good Friday, April 9, however, she capitulated to military pressure and ordered six thousand men mustered at Dover. The next day she infuriated everybody by rescinding the command, but on Easter Sunday again reversed her position, and on the thirteenth actually signed Essex's commission to lead an expeditionary force. Even so she continued to hold the Earl in check, waiting for guarantees from France. The following day she dared delay no longer and wrote Essex: "Go you on, in God's blessed name" lest "for lack of timely aid" the port be lost, but she could not refrain from adding "do in no wise peril so fair an army for another Prince's town." She need not have feared for her precious troops; ere the Earl could set sail, the cannonading that all could hear at Dover suddenly ceased and an ominous silence fell over Calais.

Elizabeth had been grasping and Calais had fallen to the Spanish, but Providence nevertheless was forgiving. The men and equipment gathered for the relief of Calais had in fact been in readiness for a far more daring attack on Cadiz. Against all reason the expedition became a storybook adventure of heroism, histrionics and incredible good luck. Even the postponement of the sailing date because of the Calais interlude turned out to be a blessing in disguise, because the entire Spanish West Indian fleet — thirty-six loaded merchantmen — was caught sitting in the inner harbor of Cadiz while all but four of its escorting galleons were off refitting at San Lucar. While Raleigh stood exposed on the deck of the *Warspite* and ordered his buglers to answer Spanish guns with the blare of trumpets, the English fleet engaged the enemy and won a smashing victory; Essex, beating time on his drum, waded ashore at the head of two thousand men and scaled the city walls; and by nightfall Cadiz was English. Unfortunately, however, the jubilant victors forgot to guard the helpless merchant fleet, and Medina Sidonia had the last word: with exquisite disdain he ordered every vessel burned, and nearly twelve million ducats worth of merchandise went up in flames.

Elizabeth was not pleased. Her heroes had attained honor aplenty and she publicly avowed that "I care not so much for being Queen, as that I am sovereign of such subjects," but privately she had some very unpleasant words to say to quarreling children who played at war, whose irresponsibility had lost her a fortune and who had no comprehension of the financial facts of life, which by 1596 were grim. The Queen's coffers were empty and economic depression had settled upon the kingdom. Since 1585 the military monster had been insatiable: the Dutch front, that "sieve that spends as it receives to little purpose," had devoured 1.4 million pounds; it cost £1,200 a month to maintain the navy on a war footing; the Armada year alone had consumed £273,000; and the following year the Queen's total expenses soared to over a million pounds. Once upon a time Elizabeth had been able to flatter her image and boast to the citizens of Norwich that "princes have no need of money. . . . We come not therefor, but for that which in right is our own, the hearts and true allegiance of our subjects," but she soon learned that monarchs could not live on love alone. As war ate at her exchequer, she had to rely more and more on exactly those financial expedients and evils that would be laid at the feet of her Stuart successors — forced loans, ship money, fiscal feudalism and the sale of monopolies. Elizabeth was no "waster," but her passionate avowal that she was never "any greedy, scraping grasper" simply did not ring true. Mars was a harsh master and even Juno had to acquire the instincts of a moneylender to satisfy him. Elizabeth's subjects might be generous with their hearts, for it cost nothing, but try as she might she could never touch their purses, and by 1593 parliamentary subsidies were "less by half [what] they were in the time of her father." With four disastrous harvests in a row, plague, ruinous inflation, peasant riots and famine, it is little wonder that Gloriana bartered long-term solvency for immediate survival and sold crown lands valued at £800,000 — a fourth of her patrimony — or that Robert Cecil confessed that "receipts are so short of the issue that my hair stands upright to think of it."

Philip of Spain had vowed that he would pawn his candelabra and "spend his candle to the socket" to be revenged upon Elizabeth. In their race towards bankruptcy he discovered in Ireland England's ulcer that would bleed £2,410,000 from his sister-in-law's treasury before her troops successfully crushed Spanish-fed rebellion. From the moment Norman barons had been urged by medieval kings to satisfy their greed for land and carve out their own petty principalities in that rain-drenched quagmire of barbarism called Ireland, there had been nothing but trouble for the English. Celtic chieftains took kindly to neither Anglo-Norman authority nor culture, and as the centuries passed English rule grew increasingly tenuous. The conquerors themselves became more Irish than English and Anglo-Saxon influence was soon limited to a beleaguered area west and north of Dublin. Elsewhere English monarchs exercised only the most minimal suzerainty, requiring tribal chiefs to pay them homage but leaving them to their impenetrable bogs and savage slieves. Rebellion had been endemic for centuries, but after the Reformation religious bigotry and Spanish gold so fired the embers of racial antipathy that it was only a matter of time until Ireland found a national hero who could rise above clan violence and lead Irish Catholics against English Protestants. Ironically Ireland's savior turned out to be an intelligent and charming Ulster chieftain who had been educated and trained in Leicester's household, was skilled in English military technology and actually held an English title — the Earl of Tyrone — conferred upon him by the Queen for his loyalty to her government. Inaugurated head of the paramount clan of O'Neill in 1593, he proceeded five years later to administer the worst beating any English army had experienced since the fall of Calais. Even as Elizabeth mourned the death of devoted old Burghley she received the news of Yellow Ford, where on 14 August, 1598, an English marshal, thirty officers and thirteen hundred men had been killed and seven hundred more had deserted.

Yellow Ford was a disgrace which catapulted the Queen into unwonted action. She had but one answer to a base Irish kern who boasted himself "so famous a rebel": she wanted him hanged even at the risk of bankruptcy. Five years later "the rules of her own princely judgment" were rewarded — "the O'Neill" surrendered unconditionally, asking only for his life. The Earl of Tyrone kept his head, much to the Queen's disgust, but the leader of the English troops was not so fortunate, for Ireland proved to be the Earl of Essex's long overdue nemesis.

The collapse of English authority in Ireland brought Essex running to the council chamber, where he staged a scene that was becoming disturbingly common — he argued furiously with everybody including Elizabeth over who was to revenge Yellow Ford. The real issue, however, was not who would risk his career in that island of lost reputations where the Earl's own father had died broken in health and wealth, but who would inherit Lord Burghley's political empire and arrange the final answer to the question Elizabeth still refused to resolve — the succession. The reign was running out, and two men — Burghley's second son, Sir Robert Cecil, crooked of back but keen of mind, and Elizabeth's flamboyant favorite, Robert Devereux, second Earl of Essex — sought to shape a future in which the old must of necessity give way to the new. The two Roberts were as different in political style and training as they were in appearance. Cecil had been carefully schooled in how to follow the political thread through the labyrinth of Elizabeth's court. By 1596 he had been a member of Parliament for eleven years, a privy councillor and unofficial Principal Secretary for five years, and was "joined in power and policy" with his father. Like father, like son, Cecil was willing to remain in the shadows, "his hands full of papers and head full of matters." Possibly he kept more from his royal mistress than his father had considered safe or expedient, but he never thwarted the Queen's authority in the one area she deemed most crucial, her popularity. It is deceptively easy to cast Cecil, with his deformed body, spindly legs and large soulful eyes set in a sallow, immobile face, as the weasel of late Elizabethan politics. He survived the transition from the sixteenth to the seventeenth century and prospered even more under lax, repellent James Stuart than he had under strait-laced Elizabeth Tudor, while the peacocks of the court, Essex and Raleigh, were destroyed. For all their gaudy plumage peacocks have the unattractive voice of a cormorant, and Essex and Raleigh were too busy strutting and feeding their insatiable conceit to realize that style was not enough. It could not substitute for that delicate amalgam of attention to detail, flexibility of means, critical analysis and consideration for others which produces great leadership. Essex and Raleigh destroyed themselves without undue assistance from Cecil.

Robert Devereux was born with many faces. Some saw a

charming, moody man, slightly fey but above all else honorable. Others described a damnably proud and pathologically touchy devil, so inordinately blind to the realities of Elizabethan politics that he did little except blunder about in an hysterical world of his own fantasy, battling windmills and blaming his failings upon the evil machinations of others. Today it is fashionable to depict simply a pathetic victim of a fate which decreed that his health and mental stability be undermined by syphilis, his pride be stung by a political system which required that he perpetually sing for his supper but never permitted him to retire into private life, and his aspirations be blocked by an older generation which refused to die. Whatever the truth, Essex lacked the cardinal quality for success at court; he was a bad judge of character, especially Elizabeth's, for he never perceived that "princes may be led but not driven." Almost from the moment he appeared at court in 1587, capitalizing on his good looks and prospects as Leicester's stepson, Essex sought not only to monopolize the Queen's company but also her bounty, which he accepted as his right to receive, not as her favor to give, and which he used to exalt not her crown but his own masculine, aristocratic prerogative. He was, observed the French Ambassador, "a man who in no wise contents himself with a petty fortune and aspires to greatness," and he found it impossible to accommodate pride to total dependence upon a sharp-tongued harridan who owned everything he possessed except his ancient lineage and manly honor. Essex lived as he died, bankrupt and mortgaged to the Queen, and the further into debt he sank the more necessary it became to prove that his fragile financial existence was sustained by solid evidence of political patronage. Consequently the Earl was forever demanding: could Francis Bacon have the post of Attorney General, William Davison be reinstalled as Principal Secretary, Sir Edward Wotton have a peerage, Sir Henry Unton a sinecure, and could Essex himself be given Burghley's lucrative office of Master of the Court of Wards, the fattest political and financial plum at the Queen's disposal.

Essex failed on every count, in part because the Queen, though she delighted in his youth, looks and silver tongue, never completely trusted his judgment or his motives, and in part because he never learned to present his case in terms she understood. When Robert Cecil advised that he persuade Elizabeth to give Bacon the lesser position of Solicitor General as being more suitable to the man and "of easier digestion to her Majesty," Essex unwittingly wrote his political epitaph by scornfully replying: "Digest me no digestions. For the attorney-ship . . . I must have, and in that will I spend all my power, weight, authority and amity, and with tooth and nail defend and procure the same for him against whomsoever. . . ."

The struggle between Sir Robert Cecil and the Earl of Essex was cruelly unequal, for Sir Robert had been specifically taught by a father who knew the importance of digests and digestions, lucid summaries and carefully weighed pros and cons. No matter in what order the two men entered the revolving door of court politics Cecil always managed to come out first, and by the fall of 1598 Essex was financially and politically desperate. The Queen had not forgotten nor entirely forgiven the lèse majesté of the previous July, when she had slapped his face for his defiant pigheadedness and he had reached for his sword, stormed out of the room, and written those portentous words about a prince's error and a subject's wrong. Deeply angered, she informed him that she would stand upon her own "great-ness as he hath upon his stomach." A showdown could not be long delayed, and Essex, knowing full well the terrible risks, but boasting that "the fairer choice" was to command armies than abide the humors of the court, nominated himself as Lord Lieutenant of Ireland.

It was a dangerous appointment for both Gloriana and her Earl, but Elizabeth believed in aristocratic leadership irrespective of competence or training, and Essex had faith in his stars. He set sail for Ireland on 27 March, 1599, at the head of the largest English army ever sent into that island of "naked rogues in woods and bogs whom hounds can scarce follow and much less men." The Queen was lavish with her instructions, prescribing exactly how Essex was to order his troops, prepare his campaign and defeat Tyrone. As usual she might have spared herself the trouble; once out of her sight Essex ignored her commands and did exactly as he pleased with disastrous results. The summer slipped by with nothing accomplished, his army withered away, and instead of making war on Tyrone he made a peace which smelled suspiciously of treason. In letter after letter Elizabeth poured out her scorn for Essex's military incompetence and his "slender judgment"; he could no more trust a traitor "upon oath," she said, than he could "trust a devil upon his religion."

Wherever the Lord Lieutenant looked there was nothing but "discomforts and soul's wounds," and in his misery he cast discretion to the winds, broke the Queen's explicit orders not to return home and left his command, gambling that if he could but speak to his princess in person and exercise his charm, the fairy-tale world in which he lived would miraculously right itself. The meeting was inauspicious. On the morning of September 28, 1599, he broke into the royal bedchamber unexpected and unannounced, to find Gloriana at her most vulnerable with her cosmetic mask unprepared and her wig laid aside. Here was no Fairy Queen but a wrinkled, ruthless old woman who sensed in her Essex not only disobedience but "popularity," and as the day progressed her ire mounted. The time had finally come to "break his will and pull down his great heart," and two days later she ordered his arrest. This time Essex escaped trial for treason, but he was banished from court, and the following autumn Elizabeth cut off the one source of income that was essential to his political and social existence; she refused to renew his license to farm the customs on sweet wine, worth £2,500 a year. Exiled from politics and faced with financial collapse, "shaming, languishing, despairing" Essex was forced to grovel, and in begging letter after begging letter he ate humble pie. His "soul" cried out "for grace, for access, and for an end to this exile," and in eloquent phrases he wrote that until he might "appear in your gracious presence, and kiss your Majesty's fair correcting hand, time itself is a perpetual night, and the whole world but a sepulchre unto your Majesty's humblest vassal." It was a pretty piece of prose but totally ineffectual. Elizabeth refused to renew the grant, and Essex turned from supplication to treason.

"The haughty spirit knoweth not how to yield" was Sir John Harington's sound sixteenth-century explanation for Essex's treason; the evil man, not society, was at fault. Francis Bacon agreed and warned the Earl that he was "ever sorry that your Lordship should fly with waxen wings, doubting Icarus' fortune"; subjects whose ambitions soared to forbidden heights were doomed to destruction. Elizabeth put it more prosaically: "Those who touch the sceptres of princes deserve no pity." Essex received neither pity nor support when on Sunday morning, the eighth of February, 1601, he endeavored to raise the unwashed multitude against his sovereign lady only to discover that subjects' love was a monopoly of the crown.

Essex did not stand alone. Joined in sedition were eight impecunious peers, all filled with bitterness against their prince, and an array of disappointed office-seekers, landless knights and paramilitary family retainers and henchmen: in effect the flotsam and jetsam of Tudor society which floated unwanted and unsalvageable upon the surface of public life.

The rebellion never had a chance. It was limited to a handful of political malcontents, lacked economic and social grassroots, and was so completely without plan and leadership that instead of marching on the court and seizing the person of the Queen, Essex and his comrades-in-arms paraded about the streets of London and ended by enjoying a three-hour noonday dinner in a Fenchurch Street tavern. In all the revolt lasted scarcely a day, and by ten of the evening Essex was safely behind bars. The Earl, as he confessed, owed "God a death." He had denied the divinity that enshrined the Tudor throne and had led others into the "infectious sin" of offending both heaven and earth. There could be only one verdict, and on February 24, 1601, he paid the price of treason on Tower Hill, where he died "in humility and obedience." It had taken the ax to do it, but Gloriana had humbled yet another "haughty spirit" and had finally taught her Essex "better manners."

Elizabeth took less than a week to sign the Earl's death warrant, a new record and grim evidence that she had few doubts as to the justice or necessity of his death. The reign might be running out, but while it lasted she would continue to have "but one mistress and no master" within her realm. No one in 1601 would have dreamed of voicing what her cousin Francis Knollys had dared to say back in 1569 — "It is not possible for your Majesty's faithful councillors to govern your estate unless you shall resolutely follow their opinion in weighty affairs." It was serious that the old charm had failed to hold the loyalty of the likes of Essex, but there was still plenty of magic left, as the Queen proceeded to demonstrate during the remaining years of her life.

The world was passing Elizabeth by, but in Parliament at least the more things changed the more they remained the same. In Commons the spirit of free enterprise was replacing the spirit of godly love in the struggle to restyle society and

GOOD MISTRESS—DREAD SOVEREIGN ✦ 211

destroy the Tudor state, but the methods still involved blackmailing the Queen by withholding parliamentary subsidies.
The danger to her prerogative was just as great when, in
November of 1601, capitalists attacked the crown's right to
grant monopolies and regulate the economic life of the kingdom as it had been when Puritans had tried to overthrow the
religious settlement of 1559. The granting of import-export
licenses and manufacturing patents on everything from the
importation of wine to the production of saltpeter seemed outright exploitation to merchants and landed country gentlemen,
suffering from soaring prices, prolonged agricultural recession
and wartime taxes. The issue was a delicate one for it struck
at the Queen's popularity as well as her prerogative, both of
which Elizabeth watched over with extreme care. Sensing that
"the prince's prerogative and the subject's privilege are solid
felicities together but empty notions asunder," Gloriana put
on her last and most polished parliamentary performance. She
offered to abolish most of the offending monopolies on her own
authority; she issued a proclamation listing the canceled licenses; and on November 30 she invited the delighted members
of the Lower House to Whitehall to hear what was ever after
described as her "golden speech."

Time had not dulled Elizabeth's oratory, and she was in full
voice. Her address was packed with oft-used phrases and her
most cherished words. "There is no jewel, be it of never so
rich a price, which I set before this jewel: I mean your love."
"That my grants should be grievous to my people . . . our
kingly dignity shall not suffer it." "I have ever used to set the
Last-Judgment Day before mine eyes, and so to rule as I shall
be judged to answer before a higher Judge." "Though you
have had and may have princes more mighty and wise sitting
in this seat, yet you never had nor shall have any that will be
more careful and loving." It was the oratorical zenith of her

reign, and with perfect dramatic timing she concluded by asking "you, Mr. Comptroller, Mr. Secretary, and you of my Council, that before these gentlemen go into their counties, you
bring them all to kiss my hand."

At sixty-seven Elizabeth could still be magnificent, and
though Cecil and others knew the truth that lay behind rouge
pot and false hair, it was nevertheless difficult to believe that
Gloriana would not last forever. She did not look or act her
years. Erect, tireless and majestic, she never let down the mask
of royalty or made concessions to age or pain. Once when told
by her cousin Lord Hundson that it was "not meet for one of
her Majesty's years to ride" in stormy weather, she angrily
replied, "My years! Maids, to your horses quickly!" For the
next two days she did nothing but scold her cousin for his
tactless suggestion. Elizabeth had what a later age would call
"bottom," and not long before her death, as one admiring
observer wrote, "she was divers times troubled with gout in her
fingers whereof she would never complain, as seeming better
pleased to be thought insensible of the pain than to acknowledge the disease. And she would often show herself abroad at
public spectacles, even against her own liking, to no other end
but that the people might the better perceive her ability of
body and good disposition. . . ." No matter the cost, the show
had to go on. There was no doubting her authority and no
need of the warning that "in old and infirm years" a prince
"may be ruled over by a new train of hungry councillors."
Robert Cecil lived in awe of his mistress and maintained that
he knew "not one man in this kingdom that will bestow six
words of argument to reply, if she deny it." Her godson
Harington was even more terrified of his sovereign and confessed "in good sooth I feared her Majesty more than the rebel
Tyrone"; he wished he had never accompanied Essex on his
ill-starred Irish campaign or received a knighthood at his

hands. "When obedience was lacking," he said, there was "no doubtings whose daughter she was." After fifty-three years the Henrician model still held good; the father lived on in his daughter.

Perhaps the old man's temperament was in fact "asserting itself in her," but if so, his charm and magnetism also leapt the generational divide. Fearful as John Harington was of his godmother, he nevertheless acknowledged that "when she smiled it was a pure sunshine." Even in old age Gloriana was a consummate angler who never wearied of fishing for men's hearts. No matter how aloof and ruthless she might in fact be, she never failed to pay her subjects the compliment of being concerned with their private sorrows and petty dreams. On the occasion of the birth of the Lord Treasurer's first grandson she tactfully protested "to God, that next to them that have interest in it, there is nobody that can be more joyous of it than I am." When Lady Norris lost her son in battle, Elizabeth wrote one of her most moving letters. "Mine own Crow, now that Nature's common work is done, and he that was born to die hath paid his tribute, let that Christian discretion stay the flux of your immoderate grieving, which hath instructed you . . . that nothing of this kind hath happened but by God's Divine Providence. . . ." In 1597 she took the trouble to answer Burghley's thankyou note for having appointed young Robert chancellor of the Duchy of Lancaster; she ordered Lord Admiral Howard to go to the old man's sickbed and tell him "although you have brought up your son as near as may be like unto yourself for her service, yet are you to her in all things and shall be Alpha and Omega." Even her anger was touched with charm, designed to delight as well as to chastise, and the Bess who shouted out of her palace window at the frustrated carter who had called three times to fetch her luggage and each time had been told the Queen had changed her mind about leaving was

assumed a place in legend as well as in the hearts of her subjects. "Now I see," said the irritated advocate of masculine
superiority, "that the Queen is a woman as well as my wife."
In response Elizabeth screamed out, "what a villain is this!"
But she "sent him three angels to stop his mouth."

Elizabeth made no distinctions between great and small.
Burghley was her "spirit" and Essex her "wild-horse," but on
progress to Warwick she thanked the town recorder for his
speech of welcome in words just as artful as those usually reserved for lords of great estate. "Come hither, little Recorder.
They told me you would be afraid to look upon me or to speak
boldly. But you were not so much afraid of me as I was of you!"
The theatrical sham is overwhelming: the conceit of Gloriana
telling her kingdom that she was more afraid of a small-town
functionary than he was of her. Yet in the midst of the prepos-
terous was a tiny fragment of truth. It was not so much that
Bess was endowed with true humility as that she never allowed
power to corrupt either her judgment or her compassion. She
was a ruthless and calculating political egotist and she demanded unconditional surrender which, as Essex discovered,
no amount of ingrained deference to authority, political con-
nivance or respect for a magnificent performance could make
entirely palatable, but Elizabeth possessed one feature which
redeemed all else — she knew herself for what she was. Juno
was "no angel," and she confessed that she might be "unworthy
of eternal life, if not of royal dignity." The distinction was
important, for unlike her father Elizabeth kept a firm hold
upon reality. Her conscience never fell victim to the theatrical
deception of her office or became the servant of expediency.
She knew she was "a most frail substance" surrounded by a
"world of wickedness, where delights be snares." She accepted
her royal status as a marvelous dignity, but she also assured her
people after forty-three years of benevolent despotism "that the

shining glory of princely authority hath not so dazzled the eyes of our understanding, but that we well know and remember that we also are to yield an account of our actions before the Great Judge."

Gloriana moved in a world of appearances and deceptions where it was "more important to seem than to be"; behind the self-absorption, however, lay something more than empty desire for power. She never forgot that she had once been a subject, fearful and defenseless like her little Recorder. Her vision could always accommodate others, and as a consequence almost no one on whom she relied ever betrayed her. Elizabeth sensed that her ablest ministers were not without their pettiness and that "the greatest clerks are not always the wisest men." All her reign she had been surrounded by flatterers, self-seekers and fanatics, every bit as greedy for ransom and power as in the days of Somerset and Northumberland. Courtiers, as Sir Francis Bacon warned, were constantly spying into her "humours and conceits" to "second them, and not only second them, but in seconding increase them." Yet Elizabeth somehow managed to see through the deceit: "I perceive they dealt with me like physicians who, ministering a drug, make it more acceptable by giving it a good aromatical savour, or when they give pills do gild them all over."

It takes a thief to catch a thief, and no one could gild a pill better than the Queen, but the explanation of her extraordinary hold over those who suffered her lashing tongue and caustic wit goes deeper than theatrics. Her goals were not very lofty — security and quiet for herself and her kingdom so that both could enjoy the pleasant gifts that God had bestowed — but she was one of those rare rulers who anguished over means and ends and who perceived that the substance of policy is more enduring than either the language in which it is wrapped or the ideological form it assumes. Living in a century of domestic and international hypertension, she was content, as she had told Parliament, "to defer, but not reject." She saw that the quarrels that divided men and kingdoms were almost never resolved by force or policy, but were simply set aside and forgotten, replaced by more pressing and popular issues.

The very quality which infuriated Elizabeth's devoted councillors the most was, in fact, her saving grace. She might, as Raleigh said, do "all things by halves," and Sir Thomas Smith might "have somewhat ado . . . to get anything signed," but neither Raleigh nor Smith faced the responsibilities of an office in which sovereigns had not only to live with their decisions but to die with them as well; as the Venetian Ambassador said early in the reign, "Queen Elizabeth . . . declines to rely on anyone save herself, though she is most gracious to all." Both Bess and her father hated the burden of ultimate responsibility. Henry developed his own defense mechanisms, but Gloriana was satisfied with delay. She stayed the execution of the Duke of Norfolk for months because, as she told William Cecil, "the causes that move me to this are not now to be expressed, lest an irrevocable deed be in meanwhile committed." Her judgment was divine, and even at the cost of procrastination, missed chances and half-measures, it had to be protected from both human error and the arbitrary rule of men. Doubt in a divine-right monarch is a corroding disease, for it strikes at God Himself. Henry VIII sought to protect himself by never changing his mind once he had come to a decision, for those who are filled with the spirit of divinity cannot forever be shifting their grounds. Elizabeth shielded herself as far as she could by never making a decision, or at least never making one which was irrevocable.

Unlike her father, Gloriana had a marvelous sense of means commensurate to ends. She hated to use an ax where the surgeon's blade would do, for she preferred the patient to live;

a mutilated corpse could neither pay taxes nor give good service. This was why Essex's death was such a shock. Her ministers often complained that her means, or the lack thereof, were insufficient to her political purpose; that either more doctors were needed to keep the patient alive, or more surgeons required to remove the diseased member or more blood necessary to purge the body politic. Her procrastination tended to become habitual with age, but in truth it had been forced upon her from the start, for Elizabeth was a monarch who was continually at odds with her Council over both the style and the purpose of state policy. Without an outright confrontation delay was often her sole recourse. Postponement was the only way Elizabeth could exercise control in a world filled with activists, military men and enthusiasts who displayed immaculate logic and the highest motives but were devoid of humor or doubt.

Though her ends were the selfish product of her father's outmoded monarchy and of an egotism which found satisfaction in the applause accorded fine showmanship and the deference given to high office, Elizabeth never approached matters of life and death from the threadbare perspective of statistics, ideology or raison d'état. Ends, even those involving her priceless legitimacy and divinity, never totally justified the means, because Gloriana saw policy in terms of human beings, not abstractions. She possessed two sensitive and highly developed political attributes which were guaranteed to blunt the edge of tyranny — the ability to empathize, to place herself in the shoes of others, and the willingness to ask herself the one question that could curb the despotism of ideas: what if I am wrong? Though she spoke for God, Elizabeth knew that she was only human, and she never forgot what she had told a deeply concerned Parliament after her recovery from smallpox in 1563: "I know now as well as I did before that I am mortal. I know also that I must seek to discharge myself of that great burden that God hath laid upon me." The essence of that burden and the indispensable quality of her style of rule was the realization that, though protocol and law were essential to authority, government entailed more than the precise enforcement of rigid principles. The substance of justice had to encompass the individual. Against those fervent disciples of state and divine justice who wished her to be done with Mary of Scotland, Elizabeth gave an answer which is worth recording — "You lawyers are so nice and so precise in shifting and scanning every word and letter, that many times you stand more upon form than matter, upon syllables than the sense of the law." No matter how sterile and institutionalized her rule eventually became or how much a younger generation might wish their "dread sovereign" gone, her godson John Harington voiced the verdict of all who had enjoyed her rule for almost half a century when he said, "I shall not hastily put forth for a new master."

Gloriana lived on, but each day the price of showmanship grew greater, and eventually the fabric of her reign began to fail — her desire to rule. Both as a Queen and as a woman she had lived alone, but the loneliness of old age was different and ofttimes she repeated "I am not sick, I feel no pain, yet I pine away." More and more she sat in the dark brooding over the past, scornfully rejecting ecclesiastical advice to look to the welfare of her soul on the sure grounds that she had done so "long ago," and sadly confessing that "she knew of nothing in this world worthy of troubling her." She was unconcerned with death, and unlike her late brother-in-law, who had planned every detail of his funeral down to the last coffin nail, Elizabeth made no preparations for her end and was content as always to let fortune and events take their determined course. She took no part in the final discreet arrangements for her succession which time, survival and delay had finally resolved: her cousin

James Stuart, "no base person but a king," was destined to succeed her. Legitimacy had been vindicated and her conscience eased. It was time for a new master; the sands of the hourglass ran out during the early morning of March 24, 1603, and with quiet dignity Elizabeth Tudor died.

The "chain of iron" had finally broken. She had imitated the King, her father, and far surpassed him, and when she died, he died too, for personal monarchy, Tudor style, came to an end. The quality of her success is like the quality of grace, it is explicable but not describable. Against all reason Elizabeth was supremely successful, and she deserves the final "answer-answer-less" to the causes of that success. In her last justification of her foreign policy to Parliament she cast accuracy to the winds and played for dramatic effect, but in doing so she succeeded in suggesting a profound truth about herself, her monarchy and the exercise of power. "I know that some other prince — that has been wise according to the manner of the world, of high conceit, and apt to fish in waters troubled — could have cast this matter in another mould; but I proceeded thus out of simplicity, remembering who it was that said, 'the wisdom of the world was folly unto God'; and [I] hope in that respect that I shall not suffer the worse for it." Nor has she, for she has remained our mirror and our hope that men can shape society by talent and style, tact and compassion, and that the alchemy of personality can transmute base historical and biological forces into pure gold.

Bibliographical Note

Bibliographical Note

If Gloriana has made "hungry where most she satisfies," the following works may help to satisfy the appetite of those who have acquired a taste for Tudors. There is no adequate life of Elizabeth's mother, Anne Boleyn, but her grandfather and father have impressive bibliographies; try Stanley B. Chrimes, *Henry VII* (London, 1972), Jack Scarisbrick, *Henry VIII* (Berkeley, 1968) and Lacey Baldwin Smith, *Henry VIII, the Mask of Royalty* (Boston, 1971). W. K. Jordan's two volumes — *Edward VI: The Young King* (Cambridge, 1968) and *Edward VI: The Threshold of Power* (Cambridge, 1970) — are well worth the time they take to read. H. F. M. Prescott's *Mary Tudor* (New York, 1953; paperback, 1962) is a fair and sensitive portrayal, and Antonia Fraser's study of Mary Queen of Scots (London, 1969) is a delightfully partisan account of Elizabeth's difficult cousin. Biographies of Gloriana herself are legion but one remains an enduring classic, Sir John Neale's *Queen Elizabeth* (London, 1934; paperback, 1957), and anyone who wishes to follow Sir John a step further in his romance with the Queen should read *Elizabeth I and Her Parliaments* (2 vols., London, 1953, 1957). More recent, albeit no more readable, treatments are Neville Williams, *Elizabeth the First, Queen of England* (New York, 1968), Paul Johnson, *Elizabeth I, A Study in Power and Intellect* (London, 1974), Elizabeth Jenkins, *Elizabeth the Great* (New York, 1959), and Mary M. Luke's two volumes, *A Crown for Elizabeth* (New York, 1970) and *Gloriana: The Years of Elizabeth I* (New York, 1973). Lord Burghley (William Cecil) and Sir Francis Walsingham have been treated at somewhat tedious but rewarding length by Conyers Read — *Mr. Secretary Cecil and Queen Elizabeth* (London, 1955), *Lord Burghley and Queen Elizabeth*

(London, 1960), *Mr. Secretary Walsingham and the Policy of Queen Elizabeth*, 3 volumes (Oxford, 1925). The Earl of Leicester still awaits a thorough reevaluation but Elizabeth Jenkins's *Elizabeth and Leicester* (New York, 1962) is a start, and Robert Lacey's *Robert Earl of Essex, An Elizabethan Icarus* (London, 1971) is a perceptive portrait of that neurotic hero.

The histories of the reign are endless, but Wallace MacCaffrey, *The Shaping of the Elizabethan Regime* (Princeton, 1968; paperback, 1971) is a fine synthesis of the first decade; Garrett Mattingly, *The Defeat of the Spanish Armada* (London, 1959) is a masterpiece of historical writing; Lawrence Stone, *The Crisis of the Aristocracy 1558–1641* (Oxford, 1965) is a brilliant political-social-intellectual anatomy of the ruling elite; and A. L. Rowse, *The Expansion of Elizabethan England* (London, 1955) is a broad and vigorous account of Anglo-Saxon colonial and oceanic conquest. E. M. W. Tillyard, *The Elizabeth World Picture* (London, 1943; paperback, New York, 1959) and Christopher Morris, *Political Thought in England, Tyndale to Hooker* (London, 1953) are brief, provocative and essential to anyone who would seek to penetrate the Elizabethan mind, and Patrick Collinson, *The Elizabethan Puritan Movement* (London, 1967) is by far the best study of God's elect.

For all who prefer their history firsthand, the Queen's letters have been edited by G. B. Harrison, *The Letters of Queen Elizabeth I* (London, 1935, 1968); George P. Rice, *The Public Speaking of Queen Elizabeth* (New York, 1966), is a convenient but not always reliable collection of her speeches; Leicester Bradner, *The Poems of Queen Elizabeth* (Providence, 1964), is short but thorough; and the various calendars of state papers, domestic, foreign, Scottish and Spanish, are gold mines of information about Gloriana, the men and women who surrounded her, and the events of her reign.

Index

Index

A

Alençon, Francis, Duke of,
62–63, 71, 122, 125,
181–182
Alford, Francis, 148
Alva, Duke of, 135, 179
Aragon, Catherine of, 19–23,
28
Armada, 69, 168, 191–192, 193,
199
Ascham, Roger, 29, 30
Ashley, Catherine, 38–39, 55
Atkinson, Robert, 156
Aylmer, John, Bishop, 71, 72

B

Babington, Anthony, 65, 186
Bacon, Sir Francis, 14, 57, 66,
89, 93, 96, 178, 207, 209,
215
Bacon, Nicholas, Lord Keeper,
89, 118
Boleyn, Anne, 18–19, 23, 27–28
Boleyn, George, 28
Burghley. *See* Cecil, William

C

Calais, 54, 100, 109, 113, 115,
174, 200, 201

Cateau-Cambrésis, treaty of, 64,
103
Catholicism:
under Elizabeth, 104–105,
108, 139, 143, 154,
155–158, 162, 172
in France, 173
and Mary I, 44, 46
and Mary Stuart, 184–185,
186
pre-Reformation, 25
and Thirty-Nine Articles,
157
Cecil, Sir Robert, 61, 70, 78,
203, 213
character and background
of, 205, 207
Cecil, Sir William, Lord
Burghley, 12, 65, 71, 75,
81, 83–84, 97, 128–129,
203, 213, 214
character of, 89, 98, 172
compared to Dudley, 98
compared to Elizabeth,
89–92, 171, 197
death of, 196
and Elizabeth's marriage,
120, 121–123, 125, 126,
182
and foreign policy, 93, 97,
110–113, 114–115, 116,
137–138, 170–172, 175,
181, 183, 201
influence of, 15, 76–77, 92,
95–96, 108, 134, 141
and Mary Stuart, 147, 148,
149, 184, 187, 189, 190
pessimism of, 13, 90, 100,
139–140

Charles Archduke of Austria,
123, 130
Charles V, Emperor, 22, 45
Charles IX of France, 114, 115,
173, 186
Church of England:
Act of Restitution, 44
Acts of Supremacy, 24, 53,
107, 155, 156, 166
Acts of Uniformity, 41, 107
under Henry VIII, 99
Prayer Book of 1549, 41,
106
Prayer Book of 1552, 106,
108, 164
relationship to state, 153–154
Religious Settlement of
1559, 107–109, 155
Supreme Headship of, 24,
48, 53, 91, 105
Thirty-Nine Articles,
155–156, 157
Clapham, John, 83, 97
Coke, Anthony, 166–167
Courtenay, Edward, Earl of
Devon, 45, 49, 51, 52, 55
Cromwell, Thomas, 25

D

Darnley, Lord Henry, 102, 130,
136, 137
Davison, Sir William, 189
Devereux, Robert, Earl of
Essex, 12, 72, 88, 195, 201,
214
and Cadiz, 201–202
character, 205–207

Devereux, Robert *(cont.)*
    defiance of Elizabeth,
        198–199, 207
    in Ireland, 93, 204, 207–208
    postering, 177–178, 196, 197
    and sister, 75
    treason and death, 208–210,
        217
Digges, Thomas, 171–172
Drake, Sir Francis, 174, 177,
    180, 191, 196
Dudley, Guildford, 42, 50, 94
Dudley, John, Earl of
    Warwick, Duke of
    Northumberland, 41–43,
    94
Dudley, Robert, Earl of
    Leicester, 58, 72, 83, 88, 93,
    132, 142, 195
    character, 94, 115, 123
    compared to Cecil, 98
    death of, 196
    family of, 94
    marriages of, 94, 123–124,
        182
    and marriage to Elizabeth,
        63, 121, 122, 123–124,
        126–127
    and Mary Stuart, 129–130
    offices, 94–95, 98, 116, 177,
        183
Dyer, Edward, 96–97

        E

Edward VI, 31, 32, 64
    birth of, 28

    death of, 42–43
    personality of, 41–42
Elizabeth I:
    anachronism of, 59–60, 66,
        174–175
    Armada portrait, 194
    birth of, 16, 18, 23–24
    as a child, 11, 26, 27–30,
        38–39
    compared to Henry VIII,
        16, 23, 24, 27, 31, 59, 60,
        61, 62, 65–66, 74, 80,
        108, 111, 113, 115, 119,
        121, 147, 175, 213
    contrasted to Henry VIII,
        68, 70, 106, 214, 216
    coronation, 18, 47, 57, 79,
        81, 100–101
    education, 29–30
    hardworking, 81–82, 97–98,
        101
    and the historians, 3–7,
        14–15
    knowledge and languages,
        30, 62, 73, 80, 81
    and legitimacy, 43, 55,
        64–65, 67–68, 145, 176,
        184, 219
    and "love," 67, 80, 134
    and marriage, 32, 54, 61,
        118–125, 126, 127–130,
        131, 133
    and Mary Tudor, 27–28, 43,
        44–50, 51, 52, 54, 55–56
    compared to Mary Tudor,
        51, 59, 64, 77
    and her ministers, 14–15,
        63–64, 66, 72, 76–77,
        88–89, 103–104, 217

Elizabeth I (*cont.*)
  and the military, 87, 177–178
  in old age, 194–196, 197–198,
    208, 212, 213, 218
  oratory, 30, 67, 69, 80, 82, 83,
    132–133, 134–135, 163,
    165–166, 188–189,
    211–212, 219
  personality, 16, 47, 56–57, 58,
    66–67, 69, 70, 71–73,
    75, 81, 180, 186, 197,
    213–214, 217–218
  princely word of, 60–61, 63,
    129, 132, 138, 149, 157,
    184
  and rebellion, 56, 64–65,
    70, 83, 112, 115, 137–138,
    154, 174, 210
  religious beliefs, 30, 48, 60,
    61, 64, 106–107, 122,
    151, 153
  role playing and
    appearances, 40, 78,
    79–80, 189, 194, 212,
    214
  and success of, 11–15, 57,
    70–71, 73–75, 77, 78–79,
    197, 215–217, 219
  and the succession, 55, 69,
    102, 125–126, 127–129,
    131–136, 218–219
  tomb, 69
  in Tower, 50–51, 52, 69
  view of majesty, 47, 59, 62,
    66, 77, 79–80, 85, 173
  written style, 30, 53, 55–56,
    78–79, 81, 82
Essex. *See* Devereaux, Robert

F

Farnese, Alexander, Duke of
  Parma, 183, 185, 186, 192
Feria, Count de, Spanish
  Ambassador, 44, 57, 76, 80,
  118–119, 122–123
Finances, 87, 110, 175, 180,
  199, 202
  crown lands, 203
  income of nobility, 34, 94,
    140
  monopolies, 93, 211
  at succession, 100
  war, cost of, 110, 115, 175,
    199, 202, 203
Fitzroy, Henry, 19–20
Foreign policy, 103, 109–116,
  169–176, 178–184, 199–201
  Elizabeth's views and
    methods, 170, 173, 176,
    179, 181–182, 184
France, 22, 103, 109, 110–111,
  114, 125, 170, 173, 175,
  199–201
  Treaty of Blois, 180
Francis II of France, 114,
  125–126

G

Goodman, Godfrey, Bishop, 80
Government:
  the court, 194
  divinity of kings, 26–27, 59,
    62–63, 74, 148, 160, 216
  factions, 95–97, 126, 140
  the household, 86–87

Government *(cont.)*
  membership of, 86–87,
    103–104
  nature and theory of, 18,
    24, 33–34, 41, 45–46, 59,
    61–62, 73–74, 78, 93, 100,
    189, 198, 216, 217
  prerogative, 131–132,
    133–134, 145, 158–159,
    211
  responsibility for, 14–15, 64,
    76–77
  See also Finances;
    Parliament
Grey, Catherine, 65, 102, 127,
  128–129
Grey, Jane, 36, 37, 42–43, 50
Grey, Mary, 65, 102
Grindal, Edmund, Archbishop
  of Canterbury, 160–161,
  164
Guise, house of, 103, 111, 114,
  184–185
Guise, Mary of, 102, 109, 113

H

Harington, Sir John, 77, 81,
  209, 218
Hatton, Sir Christopher, 88,
  190, 195, 196
Hawkins, Sir John, 180, 196
Hayward, Sir John, 79
Heath, Nicholas, Archbishop
  of York, 98–99, 105
Henry II of France, 103, 110,
  125
Henry III of France, 191

Henry IV of France (Navarre),
  65, 81, 119, 199–210
Henry VIII:
  compared and contrasted to
    Elizabeth, 16, 23, 24, 27,
    31, 59, 60, 61, 62, 65–66,
    68, 70, 74, 80, 106, 108,
    111, 113, 115, 119, 121,
    147, 175, 213, 214, 216
  death and will of, 30–32, 43,
    55
  personality of, 25
  and Reformation, 19–25, 76
  wives of, 18, 28–29
Hepburn, James, Earl of
  Bothwell, 137
Herbert, William, Earl of
  Pembroke, 87–88
Hertford. *See* Seymour, Edward
Howard, Charles Lord, 213
Howard, Thomas, 4th Duke
  of Norfolk, 112, 132,
  140–143
  and conspiracy, 143–144
  death of, 147
Howard, Lord William, 50, 88

I

Ireland, 174, 177, 183, 203–204,
  208
Ireland, George, 71

J

James VI of Scotland, 130,
  137, 162, 176, 191, 205

K

Knollys, Sir Francis, 61–62, 74,
     88, 144, 159–160, 196, 210
Knox, John, 91, 102, 110, 145

L

Leicester. See Dudley, Robert
Lennox, Margaret, Countess
     of, 102

M

Margaret (Tudor), Queen of
     Scotland, 31, 102
Mary I, 42–57
     Catholic restoration, 44, 64
     death of, 56–57, 99
     under Edward, 44
     funeral, 104
     marriage of, 32, 45, 53
     personality of, 36, 44
     and Reformation, 19–20,
          26–27
     succession of, 42–43
Mary Queen of Scots:
     and conspiracies, 143–144,
          185–186
     and Elizabeth, 52, 56, 61, 64,
          73, 111, 124, 135,
          138–140, 141, 143,
          145–149, 173, 186–187,
          188
     in France, 53–54, 126
     marriage of, 129–130
     in Scotland, 126, 136–137

and the succession, 102,
     125–126, 128
trial and execution of, 187,
     189
Medici, Catherine de, 63, 102,
     114, 116
Medina Sidonia, Duke of, 191,
     192, 202
Mendoza, Bernadino de, 182,
     183, 185

N

Netherlands (the Lowlands),
     174, 175, 176, 179, 181, 183
Newhaven, 115, 116, 127, 140,
     200
Norfolk. See Howard, Thomas
Northumberland. See Dudley,
     John

O

O'Neill, Hugh, Earl of Tyrone,
     204–208
Orange, William of, 181, 182

P

Parker, Mathew, Archbishop
     of Canterbury, 150–151
Parliament:
     Elizabeth's speeches to, 82,
          132–133, 134–135, 163,
          165, 165–166, 167,
          188–189, 211–212, 219

Parliament *(cont.)*
  first parliament, 118
  and marriage and the
    succession, 127–128,
    130–133
  and Mary Stuart, 145–149,
    186, 187
  and monopolies, 210–211
  and Puritans, 128, 130–131,
    154–158, 161, 162–163,
    164–167
  See also Church of England
Parr, Catherine, 29, 36–38
Parry, Thomas, 38–39, 88
Paulet, Sir Amyas, 189
Paulet, William, Marquis of
    Winchester, 87
Philip II of Spain:
  character of, 180
  death of, 63, 218
  and Elizabeth, 53–54,
    102–103, 122–123, 175,
    179–180, 191–192, 196
  and France, 113, 200
  and Ireland, 183, 203
  and Mary I, 45, 46, 51, 53, 55
  and Mary Queen of Scots,
    102, 143
  and Netherlands, 181–183
Pole, Reginald, Cardinal, 53,
    104
Privy Council:
  under Elizabeth, 87–89, 92,
    94, 189, 197
  under Mary, 46
Protestantism:
  under Edward VI, 41–42
  under Elizabeth, 100,
    105–106, 172, 185

under Henry VIII, 25–26
  See also Church of England
Puritanism:
  in foreign policy, 169
  nature of, 106–107, 150–154,
    155–160, 168
  in parliament, 128, 130–131,
    154–158, 161, 162–163,
    164–167
  and Thirty-Nine Articles,
    164

Q

Quadra, Alvarez de, Spanish
    Ambassador, 121,
    123–124, 154

R

Raleigh, Sir Walter, 77, 78,
    80–81, 93–94, 178, 192, 216
  at Cadiz, 201–202
  character of, 89, 205
  and Essex, 75, 196–197
Rebellions:
  in North, 65–66, 139–140,
    143
  Wyatt's, 49–50
Reformation, 19–24
Renard, Simeon, 46–47, 48, 49,
    54
Riccio, David, 136–137
Ridolfi, Roberto, 143–144

S

Sadler, Sir Ralph, 88, 131
Scotland, 92, 110–113
  religion in, 162
  Treaty of Edinburgh, 113
Seymour, Edward, Earl of
  Hertford, Duke of
  Somerset:
  death of, 40–41
  as Lord Protector, 33–36, 41
  personality of, 35, 41, 68
  wife, 33, 37
Seymour, Jane, 28
Seymour, Thomas, Baron
  Sudley, 35–39
Silva, Guzman de, Spanish
  Ambassador, 119–120, 128,
  139
Smith, Sir Thomas, 12, 216
Spain, 45, 54, 175, 179. *See also*
  Philip II
Spes, Guerau de, Spanish
  Ambassador, 140, 143
Stubbs, John, 71
Suffolk family, 31, 56, 65, 90,
  102, 126–127

T

Throckmorton, Sir Nicholas,
  89, 114, 124

U

Unton, Sir Henry, 98

W

Walsingham, Sir Francis, 12,
  30, 72, 142, 169, 170, 185,
  189
  death of, 196
  and foreign policy, 171–172,
  175, 176, 181, 186
War, 176–177, 198–199
  in France, 114–116
  in Ireland, 177, 203–204, 208
  nature of, 173
  in Netherlands, 174, 181, 183
  with Spain, 177, 180–181,
  183, 191, 201–202. *See
  also* Armada
Wentworth, Paul, 146, 149,
  151–152, 158–160, 163,
  166–167
Whitgift, John, Archbishop of
  Canterbury, 161, 164, 165,
  168
Williams, Sir Roger, 81
Woman, sixteenth-century
  concept of, 12–13, 30, 36,
  37, 38, 58, 68, 70, 77, 85,
  101, 139
Wotton, Dr. Nicholas, 88
Wyatt, Sir Thomas, 49–50

Y

Yelverton, Sir Christopher, 13